Mark Hix

*fish*etc.

D0320256

Mark Hix

fish etc.

the ultimate book for seafood lovers

photography by Jason Lowe

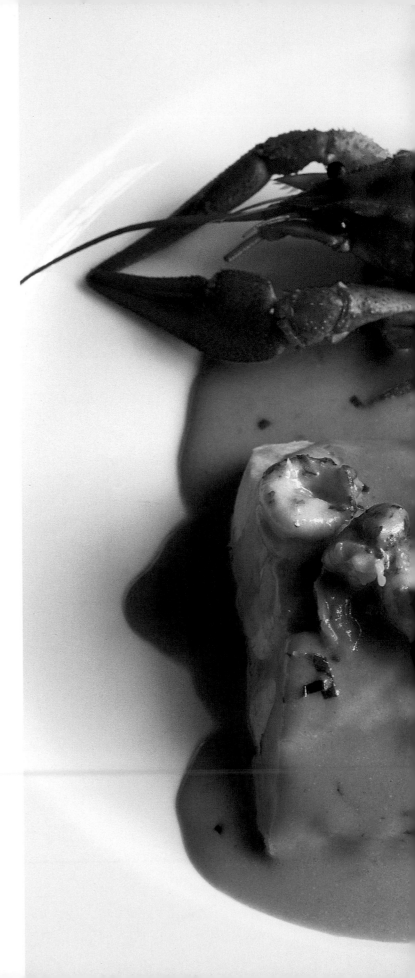

*For Ellie and Lydia in the hope that they
will grow up to appreciate fish,
if there are any left in the sea, and
to my late grandparents Bill and Ellen
who never lived to read my columns
and books.*

First published in 2004 by Quadrille Publishing Limited,
Alhambra House, 27-31 Charing Cross Road,
London WC2H OLS

This paperback edition first published in 2005
10 9 8 7 6 5 4 3 2 1

Editorial Director Jane O'Shea
Creative Director Helen Lewis
Editor & Project Manager Lewis Esson
Photography Jason Lowe
Art Direction and design Vanessa Courtier
Food Styling Mark Hix, assisted by Lee Bull, and Angela Boggiano
Production Rebecca Short

Text © Mark Hix 2004
Photographs © Jason Lowe 2004
Edited text, design & layout © Quadrille Publishing Ltd 2004

The rights of Mark Hix to be identified as the Author of this
Work have been asserted by him in accordance with the
Copyright, Design and Patents Act 1988.

All rights reserved. No part of this book may be reproduced,
stored in a retrieval system or transmitted in any form or by
any means, electronic, electrostatic, magnetic tape,
mechanical, photocopying, recording or otherwise, without
the prior permission in writing of the publisher.

Cataloguing in Publication Data: a catalogue record for this
book is available from the British Library

ISBN 1 84400 195 4

Printed and bound in China

Contents

Introduction 6

1 fast*fish* 16

2 *fish*soups 38

3 light*fish* 56

4 comfort*fish* 76

5 super-healthy*fish* 104

6 posh*fish* 128

Index 158

Where to buy fish, etc 160

Acknowledgements 160

Introduction

Although I was totally unaware of it at the time, I was extremely fortunate growing up by the sea, and not just for the fact that the coastline and beaches are some of the most picturesque in the country. I now realize that being able to pluck fish out of the ocean for free was even then – and is more emphatically now – a bit of a privilege.

Although golfing was my consuming interest from the age of eleven, something also always lured me (excuse the pun) towards the sea and sea life. My mates and their parents were all involved with fish and fishing in some way, and I just loved spending spare time on the water or at the end of the pier pulling fish out of the water. It wasn't always that easy, though. We spent many a night on a bloody cold beach with a Tilley lamp and no rewards. I guess I just liked the sea-hunter thing, and still do.

My memories of catching large pollack and being plagued with dogfish on a duff day's boat fishing didn't even influence my later career. It was much more about the sport of landing them than the desire to dish them up on a plate. Ironically, as the more popular specimens are being fished out by sophisticated factory ships, those fish that you then couldn't pay people to eat are now cropping up on top restaurant menus and being widely promoted.

You needn't worry, I'm not going to bang on too much about what you should and shouldn't eat, but I may occasionally change your views on the eating qualities of some of the less popular species, especially when prepared in an interesting way. The Marine Stewardship Council (MSC), among other charitable bodies around the world, is promoting sustainable species and endorsing fisheries who abide by the rules and contribute towards maintaining fish stocks. Many restaurants and fishmongers etc. are waking to the hard facts of overfishing and are attempting where possible to follow guidelines produced by bodies like the MSC.

In almost every recipe in the book, I have suggested other fish suitable for the same treatment, so you can make your own choices in this respect. Also, none of this should steer you away from cooking fish, as there are still many fish in the sea and lots of meals to create with them. Handled with care and treated with respect, fish can make such a wide selection of wonderful dishes.

Storing fish

First you need to identify how fresh – or how old – the fish is when you get it home. Some fishmongers these days are way ahead of the game and will pack your fish in special foil pouches that keep it cool for a couple of hours, because an hour in the back of a hot car can shorten the shelf-life of your carefully selected fish dramatically. If I'm buying lots of fish or live shellfish, I will normally take a cool box and some ice packs with me in the back of the car – a wise move when buying most fresh products, come to that.

Once you get the fish home, if you are not using it that day (though I strongly recommend you use it the following day unless it's straight off the boat), it should be either kept in the pouch or laid on a tray and fillets wrapped in cling film or whole fish put in a sealed bag. Leaving it uncovered will allow it to dry out, as well as tainting the rest of the products in the fridge. If you've seen the fishmonger fillet it, then there is no real need to wash it, as you are then just washing away valuable juices. If it's been sitting on an ice display with other fish, then give it a quick rinse under cold running water and dry it on some kitchen paper.

If you've bought too much fish and don't want to waste it, then store it in the freezer, wrapped in a freezer bag for fish pie or fish cakes, but only for a month or two for best results.

Preparing fish

I like to eat fish on the bone, although a lot of people are put off by eyes, heads and bones. The eating quality of the fish does benefit massively from being cooked on the bone, as the flesh stays much more moist and keeps a fuller flavour. A fishmonger will normally offer to prepare your fish for you, which will save you lots of time and valuable flesh, if you are not an experienced filleter.

With a pair of heavy scissors, cut off the fins and tails (and reserve them for stock or soup). Scales can be removed by scraping the skin with an old table knife in the opposite direction to that in which the scales lie. It's a messy job, so do it in the sink if possible, or surround the work area with paper or a bin liner. This should always be done before filleting, as the flesh will just get mashed if you try scaling once it's filleted.

Filleting round fish *(1-2 overleaf)*, especially larger fish, is easier with a serrated knife – not a bread knife, as such, but a carving-type knife. This gets through the bones much more easily and should leave enough flesh on the skin to eat. Start the process by removing the fish's head, then work out where the bone is and, holding the fish firmly with your non-preferred hand, cut just above the bone horizontally in clean movements until you get to the tail. Turn the fish over and repeat the process. The fatty belly can then be removed with the same knife and the pin bones that run down the centre of the fillet prised out with a pair of pliers.

Filleting flat fish *(3-4 overleaf)* is a little bit more tricky. You will need a sharp filleting knife which has a pointed flexible blade. Cut down the dorsal line (which runs along the centre of flat fish from head to tail) to the bone. Then cut with the point of the knife in sweeping movements, bending the blade on to the bone as you are cutting, until you have removed the fillet. Repeat with the other fillet on that side and then turn the fish over and repeat the process.

To skin the fillets, lay them skin side down and, holding the pointed skin at the end firmly with one hand and the knife against where skin and flesh join, move the fillet against the knife rather than moving the knife. It helps first to dip the fingers you are going to hold the skin with in coarse salt to achieve a good grip.

Preparing & cooking shellfish

You can't beat freshly cooked shellfish in their natural and simple state, simply accompanied by some good mayonnaise and brown bread and butter. Armed with crackers, a finger bowl and a glass of crisp white wine, I prefer to tackle them whole myself, whether they be crab, lobster or langoustines. If you prefer the 'no bones and mess' approach, you can buy ready-picked white and brown crab meat, and pre-shelled shellfish, although it generally doesn't have the same taste, unless your fishmonger does it for you.

The rule is that uncooked shellfish must be live and kicking (or frozen) when you buy them. Langoustines suffer a bit during transportation and you rarely see them too lively, so they are better bought precooked as the raw flesh of crustacea gets broken down by enzymes very quickly once they are dead.

1 2

5 6

3 4

7 8

Deveining & butterflying prawns *(5)* Prawn heads and shells can easily be removed just by pulling the heads off and carefully removing the shells with the fingers. Sometimes the tails are left on for presentation. Some prawns need to be deveined, as the entrail along the back can contain grit and taste a bit muddy. You can do this in several ways, depending on how you like to eat your prawns. Simply run a knife down the 'spine' just into the flesh and wash out the black entrail under cold running water. This can be done with the shells still on, using a serrated knife, but be careful as the knife can easily slip off the shell.

To *butterfly prawns* *(6)* for barbecuing and griddling you can remove the shells or leave them on. Prepare them as above, but cut almost all the way through the flesh, leaving just enough joined to act as a 'hinge', allowing the flesh to be opened up like a book (or a butterfly).

Cooking lobster   A lobster weighing 400–600g is perfect for one person as a main course and you need to allow about 8–10 minutes cooking for every 500g. There is considerable debate about what is the most humane method of dispatching lobster and crab, but with lobsters I simply follow the traditional method of plunging them into heavily salted (a tablespoon per litre) boiling water or court bouillon (page 138) and, once cooked, leave them to cool in the water or court bouillon. If I'm eating them as a cold dish, I like them at room temperature, rather than chilled. When ready to eat, simply insert the point of a heavy knife in the head first, then lever the knife through with the palm of your hand and cut the lobster in half lengthways down the body. Discard the black intestinal tract that runs along the back. Crack the claws once with the back of a knife and let your guests do the rest with the help of lobster crackers and a lobster pick (a skewer or thin-bladed knife or teaspoon will suffice).

Cooking langoustines   Like lobsters, these need to be cooked in boiling salted water, but only for 3–4 minutes unless they are jumbo 'number 1s', when they may need half as much again. Remove from the water and leave to cool. Langoustines are often sold dead but headless in order to slow decomposition.

Cooking & dressing crab *(7-8)* Again there is much debate about the most humane method of dispatching crab, but I prefer to put them in well-salted cold water and bring it to a rapid boil, then simmer for 15 minutes for crabs up to 500g and 20 minutes for larger specimens up to 900g, and 25–30

minutes for any larger. Leave them to cool in the water. If you chose to serve the crab meat out of the shell, allow 100g per person for a starter or 150g as a main course. The actual weight of the brown meat can be unpredictable, so you could buy some more ready-picked just to be on the safe side.

To get the meat out of the crab, first twist the legs and claws off, then crack these open and remove the white meat with a lobster pick or teaspoon. Now turn the main body on its back and twist off the pointed flap. Push the tip of a table knife between the main shell and the bit to which the legs were attached and twist the blade to separate the two, then push the body up and remove from the outer shell. Scoop out the brown meat and put it to one side. On the other part of the body, remove the 'dead man's fingers' (the feather-like, grey gills attached to the body) and discard. Split the body in half with a heavy knife and then split each half in half again. Now patiently pick out the white meat from the little cavities in the body, using a lobster pick or a teaspoon. Go through the white and brown meat separately to make sure there are no residual bits of shell.

If you want to make brown crab mayonnaise (for 4): put the brown meat from 2 crabs in a blender or food processor with the juice of $1/2$ lemon, 1 teaspoon each tomato ketchup and Worcestershire sauce and 2 teaspoons English mustard, and process until smooth. Add 65–75g brown bread, crusts removed and broken into small pieces, and process again until the mixture is smooth, stopping the machine occasionally to stir. Transfer to a bowl. Whisk in 2–3 tablespoons mayonnaise (page 62) and season with salt and freshly ground white pepper. Add a little more lemon juice, if necessary. Refrigerate for an hour or so before serving.

To *serve the crab meat traditionally, back in the shell* there is a definite line on the open part of the shell that will help you make the cavity larger to put the meat back into. You need to push inside this line gently with your fingers (or carefully with the end of a rolling pin) and the edge inside the line will break, leaving a neat shell. Wash the shell under warm water and pat dry. Spoon the white meat into the centre and the brown meat, or the brown crab mayonnaise, on either side (or vice versa). Alternatively, just serve a good spoonful of each on a plate with a wedge of lemon and brown bread and butter.

Preparing mussels Buying mussels can be pot luck as the meat size inside cannot really be judged prior to cooking. Generally, try to buy them in autumn and winter as, like oysters, they are then not spawning and are at their best. They can be bought already cleaned and scrubbed or you may occasionally find them a bit muddy and covered in barnacles. The cleaner mussels simply need the cotton-like beard (which attached them to the rocks) pulling off, then rinsing in cold water. If your mussels are covered in barnacles, don't worry too much. Just give them a good scrub as, once they are opened, you are only going to eat the flesh. Any mussels that are open and don't close when being handled or given a sharp tap are probably dead and should be discarded.

Preparing clams & cockles

Cockles tend to be a little more gritty than clams and will need preparing, prior to cooking as for mussels, by thorough rinsing under cold running water, giving them an occasional stir to dislodge any residual grit in their shells. Clams, on the other hand, tend to be cleaner and less gritty. They do, though, come in different shapes and sizes, and the small ones, like surf and palourde clams, are better for cooking and will be much more tender than the larger species, such as venus and quahog, which are better eaten raw or cooked and chopped. As with mussels, discard any that stay stubbornly open. If you want to eat them raw or cook them out of their shells, open and shell them like oysters (see pages 149–53).

Preparing squid & cuttlefish

Squid and cuttlefish are actually much easier to prepare than they might at first seem. First pull the head out of the body with all the innards attached, cut the tentacles just above the eyes and discard the rest of the guts. Remove the wings by pulling them from the body with your fingers and scrape away the skin with a knife. You are now left with just the body. Cut it down one side so that it is a flat piece of flesh and remove the plastic-looking backbone. A cuttlefish will normally have a much larger backbone. Once again, scrape the skin away with a knife, rinse well in cold water and drain on kitchen paper. If you are going to use the heads, first cut out and discard the eyes and beak. Depending on the size of the squid or cuttlefish, it can be cut down to size for whatever way you are going to cook it. It can also be scored in a criss-cross fashion with a very sharp knife so that it cooks quicker – you sometimes see this in Chinese restaurants.

Preparing oysters & octopus

There is information on dealing with **oysters** on pages 149–53 and on cooking **octopus** (which is normally sold ready-cleaned) on page 60.

Preserving fish

There are various ways of preserving fish dating back thousands of years to when fish was first traded for other commodities. Suitable fish were air-dried and others salted. Salt itself was expensive, so salted fish carried a high premium and was regarded as a luxury. Salt is now cheap and you can easily salt your own fish at home. Simply layer up some trimmed and boned fillets of white fish, like cod, haddock, hake, etc., with lots of coarse salt in a non-reactive container. You don't even need to go to the expense of using sea salt, as any coarse kitchen salt will work equally well. The salted fish will keep for several weeks in a cool place if you regularly drain off any liquid that comes out of the fish. It then needs soaking in several changes of water to remove the salt before cooking.

Fish bits

Apart from the obvious fleshy fillets of fish that we are all so used to, there are other delicious bits and pieces of the fish that we may not necessarily naturally request from our fishmonger. We eat meat offal like cheeks etc., so why not do the same with fish? The more obvious examples are things like herring roes and caviar, but there are some wonderful bits like monkfish liver, for example, which resembles foie gras and can be sliced and pan-fried in much the same way, or even made into a terrine. A nice way to serve it is on top of a monkfish steak with a truffle sauce or wild mushrooms, rather like the treatment given to a classic tournedos.

Cod chitterlings are another fine fish 'offal'; they are similar in flavour to herring roe but have a pork chitterling-like shape. In Spain, France and Asian countries you will find all sorts of weird and wonderful such things on restaurant menus. I will try anything and generally enjoy eating most parts of animals. Cod's tongues are tasty, come fresh or salted and can be braised, sautéed or deep-fried with all sorts of different things. Fish heads are great too, because there are so many little sumptuous bits of meat to chew on that would normally otherwise end up in the bin or cat bowl.

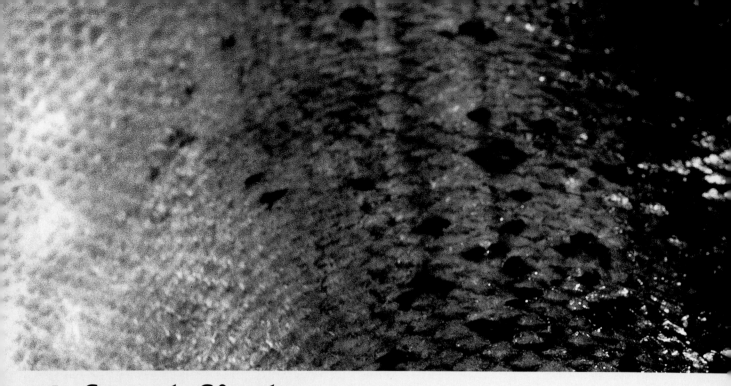

1 fast*fish*

Scrambled eggs with smoked salmon

Tucking in to a plate of scrambled eggs with smoked salmon is the perfect way to start a late lazy Sunday. It goes down very easily, especially with a glass of bubbly or a Bloody Mary. There are lots of variations on the theme, of course, like Scotch woodcock (creamy eggs on slices of toast spread with anchovy paste), and I recently discovered another, very exotic variant.

Last year I was staying at my friend Thomas's new house in Ireland and we were doing a bit of fishing on the rocks, when we saw a diving school in the harbour. We had previously spotted some sea urchin shells on the beach and got excited about the prospect of sea urchins for dinner. We naturally asked the divers if they wouldn't mind gathering some from the sea bed as one of our party had a passion for the delicious 'sea eggs', as they are sometimes known. They got us a carrier bag full of the things, which put a smile on Francis's face, and I couldn't wait to get them back to the house, despite the local fishermen's concern about their edibility. I made a couple of calls, first to Mark Edwards of Nobu, who said they were probably OK, and second to Richard Corrigan, whose homeland we were visiting. He assured me that, as far as he knew, all the species in Ireland were edible.

We ate them raw for dinner, with a teaspoon, and what was left over I served for breakfast back in the shells with buttery scrambled eggs. I literally scooped out the edible orange flesh and heated it through in a pan with a little double cream and salt and pepper and spooned it over the eggs. I remember, many years ago at the old Harvey's in Wandsworth (Marco Pierre White's first restaurant), having scrambled eggs with lightly poached oysters, topped with champagne sauce and caviar. They were memorable and quite delicious.

SERVES 4
8 medium eggs, lightly beaten
good knob of butter
2 tbsp double cream
salt and freshly ground black
  pepper
100g smoked salmon slices or
  trimmings, chopped
1 tbsp chopped chives
4 slices of brioche, each about
  1cm thick

1 Put the eggs in a heavy-based saucepan with the butter and cream, season with salt (lightly, as the fish is salty) and pepper, and stir over a low heat with a spatula until the eggs are cooked but still soft. Fold in the smoked salmon and chives and remove from the heat.

2 While the eggs are cooking, toast the brioche slices on both sides, then spoon the scrambled eggs on top.

OTHER SUITABLE FISH: anchovies, bottarga, oysters, sea urchins

Sashimi

SERVES 4

about 350g very fresh skinned
   fillet of fish, any residual bones
   removed, or shellfish meat
   (see right)

to serve
pickled ginger
daikon (white radish)
wasabi
Japanese soy sauce

Raw fish, freshly caught, is ideal for sashimi, preferably when you've just caught it on the boat and you slice it up after it has stopped wriggling. When I was a kid, I would catch mackerel by the dozen off the end of the pier for sport and if I knew then what I know now I would have gone armed with a tube of wasabi, pickled ginger and soy sauce. However, my mates would have thought I was loosing my marbles and the tourists would have thought they were in the wrong place. I do actually take these accompaniments with me now when I go fishing, together with a razor-sharp knife. Most fish and shellfish are suitable for eating raw, except for some flat fish like flounder and plaice and, even worse, skate – just imagine it! Some eat better than others and it's really very much down to personal preference. The thought of raw sea urchin is quite repulsive to some people and to others it is heavenly.

On a trip to Tokyo a couple of years ago, our first meal went by the name of 'dancing' prawns. Live prawns were fished out of the tank, peeled in front of us and we ate the flesh while they deep-fried the shells as a second course. Even for those who like prawns, perhaps the thought of live flesh wriggling about on your tongue is enough to make you heave. For many people, though, eating

sashimi is a bit of a daring eating game. For instance, I've always fancied serving chilled miso soup with live elvers.

Raw fish can also be turned into interesting salads with raw seaweeds, such as samphire, wakame, hijiki or arame. Some of these seaweeds are available in mixed packets in Oriental supermarkets or health-food stores. Pickled ginger and daikon (white radish) are useful to cleanse the palate between different fish. The quality of wasabi varies dramatically from tasteless, unappetizing-looking cheap dull green stuff in tubes to the ultimate fresh root, which can be grated on little handmade sharkskin graters. Japanese soy sauce differs from other varieties in that it is much more refined, lighter and complements raw fish without destroying the flavour.

Allow about 90g skinned fish fillet per person, remove any residual bones and rinse away any blood. With a really sharp knife, cut the fish fillets across at an angle into slices about 3mm thick and 2.5cm wide. Arrange in a neat line on a (preferably Oriental-style) platter (sitting the fish on a banana leaf can look very attractive) and serve the solid accompaniments in little piles on the plate and the soy sauce in individual bowls.

OTHER SUITABLE FISH: *most fish and shellfish, except for certain flat fish like flounder, plaice and skate*

Fish ceviche

SERVES 4

250–300g fillets of sea bass or
   similar firm white fish, skinned,
   any residual bones removed,
   and cut into 1cm cubes

juice of 2 lemons

juice of 2 limes

1 tbsp soda or mineral water

salt and freshly ground white
   pepper

for the garnish

$^1/_2$ red pepper, deseeded and
   finely diced

$^1/_2$ red onion, finely diced

1 tbsp chopped fresh coriander

a little extra-virgin olive oil
   (optional)

to serve

toasted slices of bread or tortillas

My knowledge of ceviche expanded considerably while on a fishing trip to Costa Rica. On a bit of a mission as far as this fashionable culinary oddity was concerned, I ordered it at three meals in a row. All three were miles apart in presentation and taste. Costa Ricans treat mahi mahi, sea bass and snapper to this form of brief pickling, but too much onion, citrus and coriander can overpower the fish. The third version worked best as we were left to add as much or as little of these powerful ingredients as we wished. The lemon and lime were diluted with soda water for a less acidic taste and I've based my interpretation on this. In its native South America, fish for ceviche is usually sliced. In Costa Rica, it was always cubed.

1 Rinse the fish in cold water, drain and pat dry with kitchen paper. Mix the lemon and lime juice with the soda water, season lightly and toss the fish in the mixture. Cover with cling film and chill for 2 hours.

2 Make the garnish: mix together the red pepper, onion and coriander, and add a little olive oil if you wish.

3 Arrange the fish with the juice in individual bowls and the garnish separately to be spooned over the fish. Serve with toast or tortillas.

OTHER SUITABLE FISH: cod, halibut, snapper and other firm white fish

Salmon tartare

SERVES 4 AS A STARTER

250g very fresh middle-cut fillet
  of salmon, skinned and any
  residual bones removed
2 shallots, finely chopped
15g capers, rinsed and finely
  chopped
1 tbsp finely chopped chives
juice of ¹/2 lemon
salt and freshly ground white
  pepper
pickled cucumber (page 67), to
  serve

Salmon tartare makes a refreshing and simple starter for a dinner party – or even a satisfying snack. It can be tarted up with a dollop of sour cream and some salmon eggs on top, and even pickled cucumber accompanies it well.

1 Remove and discard any brown flesh on the salmon lying just below the skin. With a large heavy chopping knife, chop the flesh finely.

2 Mix with the rest of the ingredients and season with salt and freshly ground white pepper. Add a little more lemon juice to taste if necessary. Serve dotted with some pickled cucumber and with toasted rye or sourdough bread.

OTHER SUITABLE FISH: *mackerel, sea trout, swordfish, tuna and most other oily fish*

Spaghetti with bottarga

The Italian speciality bottarga is pressed and dried grey mullet roe (*bottarga di muggine* or *boutargue* in France, where it is also widely used), and it comes pre-grated or whole in a vacuum pack. It has an amazing rich, slightly salty and bitter flavour. It's expensive, but so intense that a little goes a long way, and it serves as a good stand-by for quick lunches or suppers when you have nothing in your fridge. Although grey mullet isn't a very highly regarded fish in its own right, its roe certainly is.

1 Cook the spaghetti in salted boiling water until tender but still firm to the bite (use the packet instructions as a rough guide).

2 While the pasta cooks, heat the oil in a pan and warm the garlic through. Add the wine and butter, grate in about 15g of the bottarga and season with salt (lightly) and pepper. Simmer gently for 1 minute.

3 Drain the cooked spaghetti in a colander. Toss it with the sauce and adjust the seasoning, if necessary. Divide between the plates, grate the remaining bottarga over the top and serve immediately.

SERVES 4

325g fresh or dried spaghetti
5 tbsp extra-virgin olive oil
2 garlic cloves, crushed
2 tbsp dry white wine
85g butter
45g piece of bottarga, or more to taste
salt and freshly ground black pepper

OTHER SUITABLE FISH: *other dried fish roes, such as that of tuna*

Beetroot salad with anchovies

illustrated on previous page

SERVES 4

16 fresh anchovies, filleted,
   Nardin canned smoked
   anchovy fillets or marinated
   anchovies (see right)

500g fresh beetroot

for the marinade

100ml olive oil

juice of 1/2 lemon

1/2 tbsp white wine vinegar

2 garlic cloves, thinly sliced

salt and freshly ground black
   pepper

for the dressing

2 shallots, finely chopped

1 tbsp chopped chives

1/2 tbsp white wine vinegar

3 tbsp olive oil

This is a delightful dish made up of two ingredients that many people usually try to stay clear of. Although a day's marinating is involved, I still count it as 'fast' as the actual work involved is so quick and easy. Earthy beetroot needn't be at all boring, but most people only know it in its pickled form and never try it any other way. Anchovies come in all sorts of guises. For this dish I prefer the Nardin Spanish smoked anchovies which come in a can and have a short shelf-life, but taste like they have been freshly smoked. These are not exactly easy to get a hold of, so you could use marinated anchovies, which usually come in olive oil – or you could even marinate your own fresh anchovies. Of course, you may not be able to get fresh anchovies either, but don't be tempted to use the ordinary canned variety.

1 Anchovies can be filleted by simply running your finger down the belly and pushing the fillets away from the bone – no knife needed. If you don't fancy this, you can get your fishmonger to do it for you. Rinse the fillets in cold water, remove any visible bones that may be left on and dry the fish on some kitchen paper.

2 Make the marinade by mixing all the ingredients together. Lay the anchovies in a dish and pour the marinade over them. Cover with cling film and leave to marinate in the fridge at least for 24 hours.

3 Boil the beetroot in its skin in lightly salted water until just tender. Peel the beetroot while still warm, cut into 5mm slices and lay these on plates or a serving dish.

4 Make the dressing by mixing the ingredients together with some seasoning and spoon over the beetroot. Remove the anchovies from the marinade, wiping off as much of the marinade as possible with your fingers, and arrange them on the beetroot.

OTHER SUITABLE FISH: herring, mackerel, sardines

Skate with black butter & capers

Along with monkfish – in this country at least – skate is one of the few fish that arrives at the port ready-winged. There are various fishermen's tales as to why, but I'm not going into that. All I can say is that the edible parts of both fish represent a small part of the total body weight and it's convenient not to bother to land the whole fish.

Most people are put off skate because it is normally served 'on the bone' (they don't actually have bones, but cartilage). Although many fish benefit from being cooked on the bone, skate 'bones' are soft and easily swallowed and the flesh will simply fork away from the 'bones'. If you prefer, ask your fishmonger to skin and fillet your skate – this may surprise him or her, as it is not normal practice, except in some restaurant kitchens.

SERVES 4

4 skate wings, each about
   200–250g, skinned and
   trimmed
salt and freshly ground white
   pepper
plain flour, to dust
vegetable or corn oil, to fry
150g unsalted butter
65g good-quality capers, rinsed
juice of 1 lemon
1 tbsp chopped parsley

1 Season the skate wings and lightly flour them. Heat the oil in a heavy-based or non-stick frying pan (you'll probably need more than one) and cook the skate for 3–5 minutes on each side, until they are golden. (If you've only got the one pan, you can brown the skate quickly in it on each side one after the other and finish them in the oven preheated to 200°C/gas 6 for about 10 minutes.)

2 When the wings are almost cooked, add about one-third of the butter to the pan to give them a nice brown colour. When they are done, remove them from the pan and keep them warm.

3 Wipe the pan with some kitchen paper, add the rest of the butter and heat it gently until it begins to foam. Add the capers, lemon juice and parsley, and remove from the heat.

4 Put the skate on warmed plates and spoon the contents of the pan evenly over the top. Serve with spinach and good buttery mash.

OTHER SUITABLE FISH: Dover sole, lemon sole, plaice, pollack, most firm white fish

Fillet of pollack with parsley sauce

SERVES 4

4 thick boned and skinned
   pollack loin portions, each
   about 160–175g

good knob of butter

for the parsley sauce

good knob of butter

2 shallots, finely chopped

2 tbsp white wine

150ml fish stock (page 52, or ¼
   good-quality fish stock cube
   dissolved in that amount of hot
   water)

400ml double cream

2 tbsp chopped parsley

sea salt and freshly ground
   white pepper

With cod stocks in our waters depleting, I have found pollack to be a quality eating fish. The big ones are far superior to the smaller ones, and have large-flaked flesh like a cod. So look out for thick fillets and be pleasantly surprised by the flavour and texture.

1 First make the sauce: melt the butter in a heavy-based pan and gently cook the shallots over a low heat for about 1 minute, until soft. Add the white wine and fish stock, and simmer until reduced to about a tablespoon or so. Add the double cream and simmer until reduced at least by half and the sauce is thick. Add the parsley and simmer for another minute or so to let it infuse. Season to taste.

2 Meanwhile, preheat the oven to 200°C/gas 6. Season the fillets with salt and freshly ground white pepper, and put them in an ovenproof dish. Rub them with butter and bake for about 10–15 minutes.

3 Remove and drain on kitchen paper, then serve with the sauce spooned over them and accompanied by steamed spinach.

OTHER SUITABLE FISH: *cod, haddock, saithe, turbot and other firm white fish*

Grilling, griddling & barbecuing

Although grilling and barbecuing involve indirect radiant heat, while griddling uses direct contact heat (and is actually more like a form of dry-frying), I am discussing them all here together as the considerations and effects are much the same (indeed griddling is often referred to as 'pan-grilling') and one would normally use the same types of fish for all three treatments.

All suit a wide range of fish, particularly oily fish, as these are, in effect, self-basting, as well as many types of shellfish, from half lobsters and large prawns to scallops – and don't forget seafood kebabs. Bulky items, like whole lobster and thicker whole fish, are not that suitable for such fast methods, as the outside will burn before the interior cooks through.

The secret of good cooking in all three ways is getting the grill, griddle or barbecue really hot before starting to cook. It is also important first to brush the food with a little (possibly flavoured, see overleaf) oil or butter to prevent it burning or drying out in the intense heat. The dark skin of fish to be cooked in any of these ways is normally removed and the side with the remaining pale skin is the first/only side to be subjected to the heat. Some very firm fish, like monkfish, turbot and Dover sole, can be cooked without any skin.

Grilling

Sadly most domestic grills can't get as hot as restaurant grills – the food sort of stews in its liquid – so cooking fish under a grill can be a bit hit and miss, and the skin can blister badly. I would, though, recommend heating a non-stick tray, frying pan or mat under the grill to cook the fish in, as the standard grill trays tend to stick. One thing that helps is lining the grill pan with foil, as this reflects the heat back and cooks the other side, so you don't need to turn the fish over. Alternatively, you can put the fish in one of those folding fish holders used with the barbecue – this helps get the fish nearer the grill and also eases turning. Some cookers actually have a griddle plate under the grill as well, which means you can get it really hot and have the charcoal-grill effect at the same time.

Griddling

This can be done on a ridged griddle pan that sits on the stove top in the form of a frying pan, now normally non-stick, or a rectangular griddle plate that comes as an extra on some cookers and fits over the burners. Griddling is probably the easiest way to cook fish – although you don't get the charcoal flavour of barbecuing, you do get a good result. This method really suits fish such as tuna,

1 2

3 4

where you need it quickly flashed on a high heat to keep it rare in the middle. Get the griddle very hot before adding the food and don't try to move the food until it lifts readily or you will tear it. The sear marks from the ridges can be decorative, particularly as quadrillage, where you turn the food three times altogether, rotating it by 90 degrees each time, to give a cross-hatched effect.

Barbecuing The outside barbecue method can vary depending on your barbecue. Choose one with heavy cast-iron bars and not cheap wire ones. These hold the heat and, if well maintained, will seal the fish or meat immediately without it sticking. Barbecuing can be done on some cookers which have an integral charcoal grill. Again, the right high temperature is critical, so get the coals going well ahead and wait until the flames have died down and the glowing-hot coals have a fine grey dusting of ash. Throwing suitable herbs on the coals during cooking can imbue the fish with a lovely herby flavour.

Marinades and accompaniments For a *simple quick marinade (1)* for firm-fleshed fish (like turbot, brill, swordfish, tuna etc.) about to be grilled: mix 4 tablespoons of olive oil, 1 teaspoon of chopped thyme leaves, 1 teaspoon of finely grated lemon zest and some sea salt and freshly ground black pepper. Rub this mixture all over the fish just before grilling.

The easiest way to dress grilled, griddled or barbecued fish is with a *herb butter (2)*. Mix about 250g softened butter with salt and pepper, lemon juice if you like and chopped herbs of choice (parsley, chervil, chives, dill), roll into a cylinder in a sheet of foil or greaseproof paper and chill. Cut off discs of the butter as you need them and pop on top of the fish to serve. You can vary the flavourings in lots of ways, adding chopped deseeded chillies or a good pinch of cayenne pepper or a few drops of Tabasco. Alternatively, add some chopped shallots that have been sautéed in a little butter.

You can also make a *chilli salsa (3)* by heating 2 tablespoons of olive oil in a pan and gently cooking a finely chopped shallot and deseeded chilli and sweet red pepper for 1 minute on a medium heat. Off the heat, stir in the finely grated zest of $1/2$ lime and 2 teaspoons of sweet chilli sauce with seasoning to taste.

For a *salsa verde (4)* to serve with grilled fish: blend to a coarse purée 30g each mint leaves, parsley leaves, green basil leaves and rinsed capers with about 100ml extra-virgin olive oil, 1 peeled crushed garlic clove, 2 teaspoons of Dijon mustard, 6–8 anchovy fillets (optional) and some salt and pepper (careful, as the anchovies are salty). You may need to add a little more olive oil to bind the herbs.

Grilled Dover sole with béarnaise sauce

Despite its high price, Dover sole is one of the best-selling fish on restaurant menus. It's perfect if you want something simple, light and clean to eat, but do expect to pay double what you would for a portion of normal fish.

1 First make the béarnaise sauce: place the vinegar, shallot, herbs and peppercorns in a saucepan with 3 tablespoons of water and reduce the liquid by boiling for a few minutes until there is no more than a dessertspoonful. Strain through a sieve and leave to cool.

2 In a small pan, melt the butter and simmer for 5 minutes. Remove from heat, leave to cool a little, then pour off the pure butter where it has separated from the whey. Discard the whey. Clarifying the butter like this helps to keep the sauce thick.

3 Put the egg yolks in a small bowl (or double boiler if you have one) with half the vinegar reduction and whisk over a pan of gently simmering water until the mix begins to thicken and become frothy. Slowly trickle in the butter, whisking continuously – a hand-held electric whisk helps. If the butter is added too quickly the sauce will separate. When you have added two-thirds of the butter, taste the sauce and add a little more, or all, of the remaining vinegar reduction. Then add the rest of the butter. The sauce should not be too vinegary, but the vinegar should just cut the butter's oiliness. Season, stir in the chopped herbs, cover with cling film and set aside in a warm – not hot – place.

4 Preheat a grill or griddle. Lightly dust the skin side of the fish in seasoned flour, pat off excess and dip both sides in olive oil on a large shallow plate. When grill or griddle is smoking-hot, cook the fish, flesh side towards the heat first, for about 4–5 minutes, then turn and cook the other side for the same time. If using a griddle, you can give them quadrillage markings, by turning them 3 times after 2–3 minutes each time and turning the fish by 90 degrees each time to get criss-cross searing. Whether grilling or griddling, you may have to cook in batches.

5 Serve the fish with the béarnaise sauce. If necessary, the sauce can be reheated over a bowl of hot water and lightly whisked again.

SERVES 4

4 Dover soles, each about 500g,
   black skin removed
flour, for dusting
olive oil for coating

for the béarnaise sauce
3 tbsp white wine vinegar
1 small shallot, chopped
a few sprigs of tarragon
1 bay leaf
5 white peppercorns
200g unsalted butter
3 small egg yolks
salt and freshly ground white
   pepper
1 tbsp chopped tarragon
1 tbsp chopped chervil or parsley

OTHER SUITABLE FISH: chicken turbot, dab, flounder, lemon sole, megrim, slip sole, witch

Prawns piri piri

We now have a wide range of prawns on offer in most good fishmongers, although many still just offer those black-headed pre-cooked frozen things that give prawns a bad name. Prawns freeze well in their raw state and this allows fishmongers to offer us everything from the giant Mozambiques (which can weigh almost as much as a small lobster) down to various-sized tiger prawns and the tiniest brown shrimps or *crevettes grises*.

Try to buy the largest prawns that you can find for this – in my experience good frozen ones are reasonably priced in Asian supermarkets. Some say prawns from cold waters have a better flavour, but I have never really been convinced of this; certainly I do know that I prefer sea water prawns to those from fresh waters.

If you are squeamish about heads on prawns, then remove them or buy headless ones. Shellfish lovers, though, do generally like to enjoy every part of the fish they can.

Piri piri is an Angolan name for a type of small hot chilli, and the term came to be used all over the Portuguese empire for hot dishes, usually of fish and meat, prepared this way.

SERVES 4

about 750g-1kg large prawns, preferably still with their heads and shells

45g (or more to taste) mild red chillies

1/2 red pepper, deseeded

4 tbsp olive oil

good pinch of salt

lemon or lime wedges, to serve

1 If, like me, you prefer leaving the shells on, with a sharp serrated knife simply cut into the body along the back of the prawn to reveal the black vein. Rinse the prawns carefully under cold water, running your finger down their backs to remove the black veins, then pat dry on kitchen paper. If you prefer them peeled, simply peel the body shell away, leaving the head and tail attached.

2 In a blender or liquidizer, blend the chillies, red pepper, olive oil and salt until smooth, then mix carefully with the prawns and store in a sealed container in the fridge for a couple of hours at least.

3 You can either barbecue the prawns or cook them on a griddle pan as shown. Preheat either well. For ease of cooking and turning on a barbecue, it's better to thread the prawns on a metal skewer. Cook the prawns for about 2–3 minutes on each side for medium-sized ones or a couple of minutes more for large. Turn them sooner, if they are beginning to burn (or move them to a cooler part of the barbecue). Serve with lemon or lime wedges.

OTHER SUITABLE FISH: most fish and shellfish that suit grilling

Grilled squid with chickpeas & pancetta

Squid make perfect barbecue material, and are good for a summery lunch or dinner party. The squid needs to be cleaned, leaving the body tubes whole, with the tentacles cut just above the eyes so they stay attached to each other.

1 To make the chickpea salsa, heat the olive oil in a saucepan and gently cook the shallots, chilli, pepper and lime zest for a few minutes until soft, but not allowing them to colour. Add the chickpeas, stir well and remove from the heat. Stir in the chilli sauce and fresh herbs, season with salt and pepper and set aside. If the salsa seems a bit dry, dress it with a little more oil.

2 Preheat a barbecue, griddle or cast-iron frying pan. Make a cut down the centre of each squid and open it out flat. With a sharp knife, score the body in criss-cross fashion with lines about 2cm apart. Season the squid bodies and tentacles with salt and pepper and brush with some vegetable oil.

3 Meanwhile grill, griddle or fry the pancetta or bacon until crisp. Then cook the squid for 2 minutes on each side.

4 Serve the squid with a pile of the rocket, a spoonful of the warm salsa and the pancetta or bacon on top.

Variations   Instead of making the chickpea salsa, you could serve the grilled squid accompanied by the salsa verde or chilli salsa on page 31, or even the spiced tartare sauce on page 96.

SERVES 4

4 medium-sized squid, each
  about 200g
vegetable oil, for brushing
8 thin slices of pancetta or
  smoked streaky bacon
100g rocket, preferably wild

for the chickpea salsa
about 125ml extra-virgin olive oil,
  plus more to dress
2 large shallots, finely chopped
1 small mild red chilli, deseeded
  and finely chopped
1 red pepper, deseeded and finely
  chopped
finely grated zest of $1/2$ lime
160g (drained weight) good-
  quality canned chickpeas,
  rinsed and drained
2 tsp sweet chilli sauce
1 tbsp finely chopped mint leaves
1 tbsp finely chopped parsley
salt and freshly ground black
  pepper

OTHER SUITABLE FISH: cuttlefish, razor clams, scallops

2 *fish*soups

Mouclade

This is a creamy traditional French mussel soup which was at one time flavoured and coloured with saffron, but more recently – possibly, dare I say it, due to British influence – the aromatics used have shifted towards the curry spices. You can make the spicing as strong or as mild as you wish, but remember it's a soup and you don't want to blunt the palate for the rest of the meal.

1 First, make the broth: melt the butter in a heavy-based pan and gently cook the shallots, garlic and ginger without allowing them to colour. Add all the spices and cook for another minute to release the flavours. Add the flour and stir well over a low heat for 30 seconds, then gradually add the fish stock, bring to the boil and simmer for about 20 minutes. Pour in the cream and simmer gently for another 10 minutes. Blend the broth in a liquidizer until smooth and strain through a fine-meshed sieve. Adjust the seasoning.

2 While the broth is cooking, put the mussels into a large saucepan with the white wine and cover with a tight-fitting lid. Cook over a high heat for 3–4 minutes, removing the lid and giving them an occasional stir, until they have all opened.

3 Tip them into a colander over a bowl to catch the juices and leave to cool for 10 minutes. Strain the juices through a fine-meshed sieve into the soup.

4 Remove all but 32 of the mussels from the shells. Add the shelled and shell-on mussels to the soup with the parsley and bring back to the boil to serve.

SERVES 4

1kg mussels, beards removed and well cleaned, discarding any which remain resolutely open
100ml dry white wine
1 tbsp chopped parsley

for the broth
30g butter
2 shallots, finely chopped
1 garlic clove, crushed
small piece of fresh ginger, peeled and finely chopped
1/2 tsp ground turmeric
1/2 tsp ground cumin
1/2 tsp curry powder
1/2 tsp fennel seeds
a few curry leaves
a pinch of saffron threads
1 tbsp flour
1.1 litres fish stock (page 52, or a good-quality fish stock cube dissolved in that amount of hot water)
300ml double cream
salt and freshly ground black pepper

OTHER SUITABLE FISH: clams, cockles, razor clams

Shellfish bisque

SERVES 4-6

1kg shellfish trimmings, shells, etc. (see right)

1 tbsp vegetable oil

1 small onion, roughly chopped

1 small leek, well rinsed, trimmed and roughly chopped

3 garlic cloves, roughly chopped

1 small fennel bulb, roughly chopped

a few sprigs of tarragon

1 bay leaf

45g butter

2 tbsp tomato purée

3 tbsp flour

glass of white wine

2 litres fish stock (see page 52, or a good-quality fish stock cube dissolved in that amount of hot water)

salt and freshly ground white pepper

200ml double cream

Shellfish bisque can be made from all sorts of different shellfish, from small green crabs to spider crabs, langoustines, prawns, lobster, etc. You can cook the whole fish and use the flesh in salads, etc, but with this type of soup the flavour really comes from the shells. If I'm having shellfish at home I never throw the shells away; I freeze them as they are or make them into bisque or shellfish sauce for a rainy day. It can be quite costly just buying shellfish to make soup, so such economical ruses help save some money. Bisque can be thickened in several ways, all of which give much the same results. For example, rice can be used instead of flour; it disintegrates during cooking and gets blended in.

1 With the back of a heavy chopping knife or meat cleaver, or a rolling pin, break the trimmings, shells, etc. up into small pieces (doing this in a bag saves on the subsequent cleaning up).

2 Heat the oil in a large heavy-based saucepan and fry the shells, etc., over a high heat for about 5 minutes, stirring every so often until they begin to colour. Add the onion, leek, garlic, fennel, tarragon and bay leaf, and cook for another 5 minutes or so, until the vegetables begin to colour. Add the butter and stir well, then add the tomato purée and flour, stir well and cook for a minute or so over a low heat. Add the white wine, then slowly add the fish stock, stirring to avoid any lumps. Bring to the boil, season with salt and pepper, and simmer for 1 hour.

3 Pour the soup, shells and all, into a colander set over a large bowl, stirring the shells so that any small pieces of flesh go into the liquid. Remove about one-third of the softer white body shells (prawn and lobster shells blend well but crab claw and main shells are too hard) and put them in with the liquid, discarding the rest. Blend the shells and liquid in a liquidizer or strong food processor until smooth, then strain through a fine-meshed sieve.

4 Return to a clean pan, adjust the seasoning if necessary, and bring to the boil. If the soup is not thick enough to coat the back of a spoon, simmer it until it thickens. Add the cream, heat through briefly, adjust the seasoning again if necessary and stir well.

OTHER SUITABLE FISH: crawfish, green crab, langoustine, lobster, prawns, spider crab

Vichyssoise with oysters

Since it was invented by a French chef at the Algonquin Hotel in New York in 1917, everyone has developed their own version of this chilled soup. It is also delicious hot, though the most important thing is getting the maximum flavour from the potatoes and leeks. Buy good-tasting potatoes, new or old, but either way not too waxy or you'll end up with glue. I would recommend Roseval, Maris Piper or large Jersey Royals. Don't cook the hell out of them either. Vichyssoise needs to be cooked for just as long as the potatoes take and then cooled down quickly to preserve flavour and colour.

I like to use olive oil for cold soups, as butter tends to leave solid speckles in the soup when it's chilled. The addition of the oysters gives it a somewhat indulgent feel. If you want to take this further, why not even try a spoonful of caviar?

1 In a covered pan, gently cook the leeks in the olive oil without allowing them to colour for 4-5 minutes. Add the potatoes and vegetable stock, bring to the boil, lightly season with salt and pepper and simmer for 10-15 minutes, or until the potatoes are just tender.

2 Add the spring onions and 4 of the oysters with their juices and simmer for another 2 minutes.

3 Blend until smooth in a liquidizer, then strain through a fine-meshed sieve. Adjust the seasoning, if necessary. Allow the soup to cool down in a bowl over some iced or cold water, stirring occasionally. When the soup is cold it will thicken, so you may need to adjust the consistency with a little more stock or milk as you prefer.

4 Add the potato and leek garnish and stir in well. Serve in shallow soup/pasta bowls with one of the reserved oysters in each bowl, sprinkled with the chives.

SERVES 4

2 medium leeks, roughly chopped and well rinsed

1 tbsp olive oil

250g well-flavoured new or old potatoes (see left), peeled and roughly chopped

1 litre vegetable stock (or Marigold bouillon powder or a good-quality vegetable stock cube dissolved in that amount of hot water)

salt and freshly ground black pepper

2-3 spring onions, roughly chopped

8 oysters, removed from their shell and juices reserved

for the garnish

1 small waxy potato, cut into 1cm dice and cooked until tender in boiling salted water

1/2 small leek, cut into 1cm dice, well rinsed and cooked until just tender in boiling salted water

1 tbsp finely chopped chives

OTHER SUITABLE FISH: any mollusc

Shrimp & okra gumbo

SERVES 4-6

4 tbsp vegetable oil

4 tbsp plain flour

1 small onion, finely chopped

2 celery stalks, peeled if stringy
and chopped into 5mm dice

1 green pepper, deseeded and
chopped into 5mm dice

200g okra, trimmed and thinly
sliced

1 small (220g) can of chopped
tomatoes, drained, reserving
the juice, and the flesh chopped
a little further

salt and freshly ground black
pepper

a few splashes of Tabasco sauce

for the stock

500g raw prawns, preferably with
the heads on

1 onion, roughly chopped

3 garlic cloves, crushed

1 tbsp vegetable oil

1 tbsp tomato purée

1 glass of dry white wine

10 black peppercorns

a few sprigs of thyme

1/2 tsp fennel seeds

2 litres fish stock (page 52, or a
good-quality fish stock cube
dissolved in that amount of hot
water)

Probably the best-known dish to come out of Louisiana, *gumbo* is an African word for okra, which is an essential ingredient and contributes to the thickening process, mostly achieved by a roux base and the addition of filé powder, the ground leaves of the sassafras tree. You can make this hearty soup/stew out of almost anything, for serving a main course or as a starter. It traditionally has some cooked rice in it, but I prefer it without when serving it as a soup.

A gumbo is always thickened with a dark roux made with oil and flour, unlike our butter and flour method, which seems odd to most classically trained cooks, but it works and, in fact, you wouldn't know the difference.

1 First make the stock: remove heads and shells from the prawns, de-vein them by running a knife down their backs and removing the black intestinal tract. Rinse the prawns well and put in the refrigerator.

2 Chop up the prawn heads and shells a bit and fry them with the onion and garlic in the vegetable oil over a high heat for a few minutes until they begin to colour. Add the tomato purée, wine, peppercorns, thyme, fennel seeds and stock. Bring to the boil and simmer gently for 1 hour. Remove from the heat and strain through a sieve, using the back of a large spoon or ladle to push through as much as possible.

3 Meanwhile, make the roux: in a heavy-based pan, heat 3 tablespoons of the vegetable oil and stir in the flour. Cook over a low heat for 4-5 minutes, stirring every so often, until the mixture turns to a sandy colour. Remove from the heat and set aside.

4 Heat the remaining vegetable oil in another heavy-based saucepan and fry the onion, celery, green pepper and okra for 3-4 minutes until they soften. Add the roux, stir well and gradually add the shrimp (ooops, prawns) stock, canned tomatoes and juice. Season with salt and pepper, add a few drops of Tabasco and simmer for 1 hour.

5 Add the prawn meat and cook for 5 minutes more. Before serving, adjust the seasoning, adding a little more Tabasco if you wish.

OTHER SUITABLE FISH: *crayfish (crawfish in Louisiana), langoustines, lobster or any firm white fish*

Cullen skink

SERVES 4-6

good knob of butter

1 large leek, trimmed, roughly
    chopped and well rinsed

1 small floury potato, about 200g,
    peeled and roughly chopped

1 bay leaf

300g fillets of undyed smoked
    haddock

4 tbsp double cream

1 tbsp chopped parsley

for the fish stock

2kg white fish bones/trimmings

2 leeks

2 onions

^{1}/$_2$ head of celery

^{1}/$_2$ lemon

1 tsp fennel seeds

20 black peppercorns

1 bay leaf

a few thyme sprigs

handful of parsley

salt

Cullen is the village on the Moray Firth where this classic Scottish soup originated, and 'skink' is an ancient word for a broth or soup. Traditionally the soup wouldn't have the added cream or parsley, and some modern variations even include bacon and other such heresies. This soup is substantial enough to be served as a main course or brunch dish. Avoid the yellow-dyed smoked haddock and buy the lighter-coloured natural fillets or Arbroath smokies, which are on the bone. If you haven't time to make stock, just use a good-quality stock cube dissolved in that amount of hot water.

1 First make the fish stock: put the bones/trimmings in a large pan. Coarsely chop the vegetables, rinsing the leeks well, and add to the pan with the remaining ingredients. Cover with about 1^1/$_2$ litres of cold water and bring to the boil. Skim well and simmer gently for 20 minutes, skimming from time to time. Strain and season to taste (be careful with the salt if you might be reducing the stock down in a later recipe).

2 Melt the butter in a pan, stir in the leek, cover and cook gently for a few minutes until soft. Add the fish stock, potato, bay leaf and haddock. Bring to the boil, season, lower the heat and simmer for 15 minutes. With a slotted spoon, carefully remove the haddock from the pan and put to one side. Simmer the soup for another 15 minutes.

3 Remove the bay leaf and blend the soup in a liquidizer until smooth. Strain through a fine-meshed sieve into a clean pan.

4 Remove the flesh from the haddock skin, checking for residual bones, and flake it into the soup. Stir in the cream and parsley, and bring back to a simmer. Adjust the seasoning again, if necessary, and serve.

Variation   For a smoked fish chowder, add ^{1}/$_2$ fennel bulb to the vegetables, sprinkle the softened veg with 1 tablespoon flour and cook this in briefly, stirring, then add ^{1}/$_2$ glass of dry white wine with the stock, and replace the parsley with dill. Don't blend the soup before adding the fish and cream, but remove a ladleful and blend that until smooth, then add back to the soup with the dill.

OTHER SUITABLE FISH: any hot-smoked fish

Fish soup

This is a perfect way to use up fish that's a bit too bony or doesn't have enough flesh to hold its own on a plate. Otherwise, if you are lucky enough to have a good fishmonger, he will probably sell his own 'fish soup mix', which will contain things like rascasse, conger eel, rockfish, gurnard – all the bony fish that are full of flavour. As the soup is blended and strained, the bones don't matter. You can use a wide range of fish, however, as long as you have several varieties and try to include at least one whole fish (I find snapper, gurnard or red mullet is best), but avoid oily fish. The soup freezes well, so you could make a double batch when lucky enough to have the right mix. If you don't feel up to making the rouille, just sprinkle some grated cheese, preferably Gruyère, on the toasts to serve with the soup.

1 Heat the olive oil in a large heavy-based pot and gently fry the fish, vegetables, garlic, spices and herbs for about 10 minutes. Add the tomato purée, chopped tomatoes, red wine and fish stock. Bring to the boil, season with salt and pepper, and simmer for 50 minutes.

2 Blend about one-third of the soup (bones and all) in a liquidizer. Return it to the pot and simmer gently for another 20 minutes.

3 Strain the soup by pushing it through a medium-meshed sieve or conical strainer with the back of a ladle and adjust the seasoning, if necessary, with more salt and pepper.

4 If you like, make a rouille to serve with the soup: ladle about 100ml of the soup into a pan and simmer the saffron and garlic in it for a couple of minutes. Stir in the bread, remove from the heat and let cool a little. Pour into a blender and process well with the egg yolk. Slowly trickle in the mixed oils, stopping the machine occasionally and scraping down the sides. When nicely blended and thick, season to taste with a little salt and cayenne and the lemon juice.

5 You can float a slice of baguette spread with rouille in the centre of each bowl, or simply ladle out the soup and then let everyone add the toasts and rouille themselves.

SERVES 4-6

2 tbsp olive oil
500g fish (heads, tails and all) as on the left, roughly chopped
1 small onion, roughly chopped
1/2 leek, well rinsed, trimmed and roughly chopped
1/2 fennel bulb, roughly chopped
1/2 red pepper, deseeded and roughly chopped
1 small potato (about 125g), peeled and roughly chopped
3 garlic cloves, chopped
good pinch of saffron
5 black peppercorns
2 juniper berries
1 bay leaf
a few sprigs of thyme
3 tbsp tomato purée
150g can of chopped tomatoes
150ml red wine
1.5 litres fish stock (opposite, or a good-quality fish stock cube dissolved in hot water)
salt and freshly ground black or white pepper
1 baguette, sliced at an angle and toasted, to serve (optional)

for the rouille (optional)
good pinch of saffron strands
3 peeled garlic cloves, crushed
1 thick slice of white bread, crusts removed and torn into pieces
1 egg yolk
3 tbsp extra-virgin olive oil
3 tbsp vegetable oil
cayenne pepper
1 tsp lemon juice

OTHER SUITABLE FISH: a wide range of non-oily fish

Thai fish & coconut soup

Thai herbs and spices give a delicious fragrant quality to soups, whether they are based on meat or fish. These days you can buy Thai spices quite readily from Asian greengrocers and many supermarkets.

1 Put all the ingredients for the stock into a pan with the stalks from the coriander for the soup and some salt and pepper. Bring to the boil and simmer gently for 1 hour, occasionally skimming off any scum.

2 About halfway through that cooking time, mix the cornflour with a little water and stir it into the stock. Simmer for 20 minutes, strain the stock and return to the pan. Add the coconut cream and whisk it in.

3 Blanch the shredded ginger and chilli in boiling water for 2 minutes to remove the harsh flavours. Drain and add them to the soup with the chopped lemon grass.

4 Cut the fish into rough 2–3cm pieces and add to the soup. Then stir in the spring onions, coriander and lime leaves. Bring back to the boil and adjust the seasoning, if necessary.

Variation   For a more filling soup, almost like a classic laksa, soak about 200g flat rice noodles until soft and add them to the soup at the last minute.

SERVES 8

a few sprigs of coriander, roughly chopped

25g cornflour

150g coconut cream (block or liquid)

30g fresh root ginger or galangal, peeled and shredded

1 mild red chilli, deseeded and shredded

1 lemon grass stalk, hard outer layers removed and the bulbous ends finely chopped

250g firm-fleshed fish, like monkfish cheeks, fillets of snapper or catfish

4 spring onions, trimmed and sliced at an angle

4 fresh lime leaves

for the Thai fish stock

1.5 litres fish stock (page 52, or a good-quality fish stock cube dissolved in that amount of hot water)

1 onion, roughly chopped

25g fresh root ginger or galangal, peeled and roughly chopped

1 lemon grass stalk, roughly chopped

3 garlic cloves, roughly chopped

3 lime leaves

1 mild chilli, deseeded and chopped

salt and freshly ground black pepper

OTHER SUITABLE FISH: *firm-fleshed fish, such as snapper and grouper, and most shellfish, especially prawns*

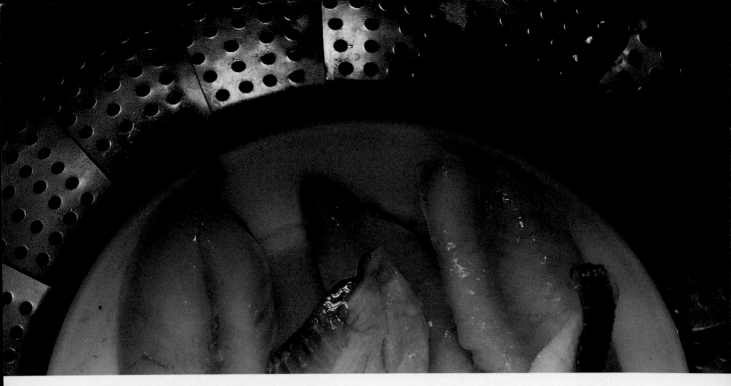

3 light*fish*

Lobster & asparagus cocktail

As with prawns, when it comes to serving lobster, sometimes the good old classic dishes – smart or otherwise – work best. You may think it's a waste of lobster making it into a cocktail, but why? If it's prepared and cooked well, you just can't beat it; while even the best and most sophisticated of lobster dishes can be messed up by bad preparation and cooking.

1 Shred the lettuce and chicory as finely as you can and mix together with the spring onions.

2 Meanwhile, cook the asparagus in boiling salted water for 4–5 minutes, or until just tender. Drain well and leave to cool.

3 At the same time, make the sauce by mixing all of the ingredients together and seasoning with salt and pepper.

4 To serve, put the lettuce mixture into small bowls, large martini glasses or similar, arrange the lobster meat on top with the asparagus and spoon the sauce over the lobster (or spoon it over the lettuce before the lobster and asparagus). Serve with lemon or lime quarters.

SERVES 4

1 small head of Cos lettuce

1 head of chicory

4 spring onions, finely shredded

450–500g asparagus, woody
  ends trimmed off

2 cooked lobsters (see page 12),
  each about 500–600g,
  meat removed from the shell
  and sliced into bite-sized pieces

1 lemon or lime, quartered, to serve

for the cocktail sauce

5 tbsp thick mayonnaise (page
  62 or good-quality ready-made)

5 tbsp tomato ketchup

2 tsp Worcestershire sauce

a few drops of Tabasco sauce

1 tbsp orange juice

1 tbsp creamed horseradish or 1
  tbsp freshly grated horseradish

1 tbsp Pernod or Ricard

1 tbsp chopped dill

salt and freshly ground black
  pepper

OTHER SUITABLE FISH: crab, crayfish, langoustine, prawns, rock lobster

Potted shrimps on toast

SERVES 4 AS A STARTER
175g unsalted butter
juice of 1/2 lemon
good pinch of freshly grated
    mace or nutmeg
pinch of cayenne pepper
1 small bay leaf
1 tsp anchovy essence or paste
200g peeled brown shrimps
salt and freshly ground white
    pepper

to serve
good-quality brown bread
2 lemons, halved

This is a nice simple starter that can be made the day – or even a few days – before and just brought out of the fridge an hour or so ahead of time to allow it to soften up slightly. Morecambe Bay, on the Lancashire coast, is the home of shrimping in Britain and many commercial potted shrimps come from there. Ask your fishmonger to order you some peeled brown shrimps, because it could take you the best part of a day to peel enough for four. They will be expensive but well worth it. If you can't find these, peeled prawns from a tub will do the job, as they have a good flavour too.

1 Melt the butter in a pan, add the lemon juice, mace or nutmeg, cayenne pepper, bay leaf and anchovy essence or paste, and simmer gently on a very low heat for 2 minutes to allow the spices to infuse. Remove from the heat and leave the mixture to cool until it is just warm.

2 Add the shrimps and stir well, then season with salt and freshly ground white pepper. Put the mixture into the fridge and stir every so often. When the butter starts to set, fill 4 ramekins with the mixture.

3 If you are not serving the shrimps that day, cover the ramekins with cling film and store them in the fridge. It is important, though, not to serve them straight from the fridge, as the butter will be too hard to spread nicely on to the toast and won't taste as good. Serve on or with hot brown bread toast and lemon halves.

OTHER SUITABLE FISH: *crab, lobster, prawns, salmon*

Octopus & potato salad with samphire

SERVES 4-6

1 octopus, about 1–1.5 kg, cleaned

125g samphire, woody stalks
   trimmed

200g waxy new potatoes, like
   Charlotte, Roseval or Anya,
   cooked in their skins, peeled
   and halved

30g capers, rinsed

for the cooking liquor

1/2 tsp fennel seeds

1 tsp white peppercorns

2 bay leaves

5 garlic cloves, roughly chopped

2 small onions, roughly chopped

2 celery stalks, roughly chopped

1 glass of white wine

1 lemon, halved

3 tbsp salt

for the dressing

5 tbsp olive oil

juice of 1/2 lemon

1 tbsp good-quality white wine
   vinegar, like Chardonnay or
   white balsamic

salt and freshly ground white
   pepper

It's unfortunate that those pre-made seafood salads that you can buy in supermarkets and jars – and that are even served in some restaurants – include baby octopuses that taste like rubber. The fresh stuff is pretty simple to cook and well worthwhile. You hear stories of Greek fishermen bashing octopuses over the rocks to tenderize them. I'm not sure if that really works, as it is the cooking that determines the tenderness; undercooked, octopus is completely inedible.

This method is simple enough, but you could also try cooking the octopus with no liquid at all in a covered pot with some seasoning for about the same amount of time. If you can't find fresh octopus, the frozen ones are fine.

1 Put all of the ingredients for the cooking liquor in a large pan with enough water to be able eventually to cover the octopus, bring to the boil and simmer gently for 15 minutes.

2 Add the octopus, bring back to the boil (you may need to put a pan lid slightly smaller than the one you are using on the octopus to keep it submerged in the water) and simmer gently for 50 minutes, or another 10 minutes for larger ones above 1.5kg. Leave to cool completely in the liquid until required.

3 Blanch the samphire in boiling unsalted water for 30 seconds, then drain in a colander and refresh in cold running water.

4 Make the dressing by mixing all the ingredients together and seasoning with salt and pepper.

5 Remove the octopus from the cooking liquor and drain it on kitchen paper. Cut the legs and body into 2–3cm chunks and put them in a bowl with the samphire and new potatoes. Season with salt and pepper and mix with half the dressing.

6 Arrange on plates, then scatter over the capers and spoon over the rest of the dressing.

OTHER SUITABLE FISH: cuttlefish, langoustine, lobster, prawns, squid

Spaghetti alle vongole

In Italy, exact recipes for *spaghetti alle vongole* vary from region to region and even from restaurant to restaurant. Some will add chilli, dried or fresh, and occasionally you will see tomatoes added, although I prefer the purist version with no tomatoes and just a hint of dried chilli. The clams used vary too and can be quite expensive. Always try to use smaller clams that cook quickly and stay tender. Carpetshell clams (*palourdes* in France and *vongole* in Italy) are classic here, but my favourites are English surf clams, which are small and oval-shaped, and are gathered in the surf, which naturally helps to clean out any grit that sometimes remains in the shell.

1 Cook the spaghetti in boiling salted water until tender but still firm to the bite, then drain.

2 While the spaghetti is cooking, heat the olive oil in a pan large enough to hold the clams and gently cook the garlic, shallots and chilli for 2–3 minutes until soft. Add the clams with the parsley and white wine, season with salt and pepper, turn up the heat, cover with a tight-fitting lid and cook for 4–5 minutes, giving the occasional stir, until all the clams have opened (one or two may not, so don't keep cooking just for them once most have opened).

3 Add the butter and the drained spaghetti to the pan, stir well over a low heat for a minute and serve immediately.

Variation   For a last-minute storecupboard treat, canned clams work really well in this dish. Look for the Italian brands actually sold as 'vongole'. Drain and rinse well, then just add them to the softened aromatics and warm through gently.

SERVES 4

350–400g dried spaghetti

5 tbsp extra-virgin olive oil

4 garlic cloves, crushed

2 large shallots, finely chopped

1/2 tsp dried red chilli

800g small clams (see left), rinsed well in cold running water

2 tbsp chopped flat-leaf parsley

3 tbsp dry white wine

salt and freshly ground white pepper

50g unsalted butter

OTHER SUITABLE FISH: cockles, mussels, razor clams

Salads, cold sauces & dressings

Fish salads are perfect for outdoor eating in the summer, whether they are based on a piece of fish off the barbecue or a freshly poached piece of fish served on some interesting salad leaves and asparagus tips or a salad of summer beans tossed with olive oil and a good dressing. Simplicity and fresh ingredients are the keys to a good salad and I love growing my own interesting salad leaves, such as purslane, land cress and a mesclun mix that you can just cut, wash and serve.

You don't always have to cook the fish for salads – if you have ultra-fresh scallops, say, they can just be sliced and dipped in some lemon juice and olive oil, seasoned and served.

For a *vinaigrette (1)* to use in a fish salad, put 1 tablespoon good-quality tarragon vinegar, 2 teaspoons Dijon mustard, 1 peeled garlic clove, 2 tablespoons each olive oil and vegetable or corn oil into a clean jar with salt and pepper. Give it a good shake and leave to infuse overnight at room temperature.

For a basic *mayonnaise (2)*, put 2 egg yolks, 2 teaspoons white wine vinegar, 1 teaspoon English mustard, 2 teaspoons Dijon mustard, 1/2 teaspoon salt and some freshly ground white pepper into a non-reactive bowl (aluminium will make the mayonnaise go grey) set on a damp cloth to stop it slipping. Mix well with a whisk, then gradually trickle 100ml olive oil mixed with 200ml vegetable oil into the bowl, whisking continuously. If the mayonnaise gets too thick, add a few drops of water and continue whisking. When all the oil is incorporated, taste and adjust the seasoning, and add a little lemon juice.

Mayonnaise makes an excellent vehicle for lots of different flavours. With fish, in particular, it can be simply converted into herb mayonnaise by adding some chopped soft herbs, such as parsley, chervil, chives and tarragon. Mixing in a little pesto makes a tasty dipping sauce for fish goujons, and the addition of wasabi is particularly good for Japanese-influenced dishes.

Dressings that suit fish, like the mayonnaise and vinaigrette, can be developed on from the basic recipes by adding herbs, etc., or by blending in some of the wonderful vinegars now available in supermarkets, shops and delis. Some of my favourites are the Spanish Cabernet Sauvignon and Chardonnay, which are pricey, but mixed 1 part to 4 parts extra-virgin olive oil they transform a salad *(3)*.

If you like to experiment with *Oriental* ingredients in your fish salads, then some crushed garlic, ginger and lemon grass mixed with soy, rice vinegar, sesame oil and chopped coriander *(4)* will go well with some of the Asian leaves and vegetables, as well as fish marinated in similar spices.

1 2
3 4

Elvers

SERVES 4

2 tbsp olive oil

1/2 red chilli, deseeded

2 garlic cloves, crushed

good knob of butter

350–400g live elvers

1 tbsp chopped parsley

salt and freshly ground black
   pepper

These matchstick-sized, almost transparent eels make a long journey from the Sargasso Sea to the same inland waters their parents came from, sometimes taking three years to do so. You don't often see elvers on menus here as their price – similar to that of the prized black truffle – puts off most diners and restaurateurs. In Spain you will find them frozen in supermarkets, but over here you will be lucky to see them unless you go to Gloucester in March to April, which is when the locals take part in elver-eating competitions. The record is 500g in one minute.

1 Heat the olive oil briefly in a frying pan with the chilli and garlic. Add the butter and, when it begins to foam, add the elvers and parsley, and season with salt and pepper. Cook over a medium heat, stirring occasionally, for 1 minute, then tip them out into individual (preferably terracotta) serving dishes.

OTHER SUITABLE FISH: any extremely small fish fry or tiny squid or cuttlefish

Herring roes on toast

Herring soft roes or milt are normally sold frozen or defrosted but can occasionally be found fresh during the spring and early summer months. The frozen ones cook quite nicely and, treated correctly, no one will know that they were not fresh. The other great fish offal is cod chitterlings, which look similar to those belonging to the pig, but taste rather like herring roes.

SERVES 4
400–450g soft herring roes
150g butter
salt and freshly ground white
   pepper
4 thick (about 1¹/₂cm) slices of
   bread (a small bloomer-style
   loaf will do)
60g capers, drained and rinsed
1 tbsp finely chopped parsley

1 Pat the herring roes dry on some kitchen paper. Heat 50g of the butter in a trusty heavy frying pan (or, better still, a non-stick one). Season the roes and cook them on a medium heat until they are golden brown – they will curl up during cooking.

2 Meanwhile, toast the slices of bread on both sides. When the roes are ready, pile them on the toast. Melt the rest of the butter in the pan, add the capers and parsley, and spoon it over the roes.

OTHER SUITABLE FISH: cod roe or chitterlings, monkfish cheeks or liver, any edible fish roes or livers

Skate in parsleyed jelly

This is a delicious way to eat skate cold and works a treat as a light lunch dish on a hot summer's day. I suppose it's a sort of fishy version of classic *jambon persillé*. Skate has a naturally high gelatine content in the bones and the skin, so do try to get all the bits with it. In case the fishmonger throws them away, I have added a gelatine leaf here just to make sure. Baby leeks dressed in a tarragon and mustard vinaigrette make a delicious alternative accompaniment.

1 Chop the skate bones into pieces with a heavy knife and put them in a saucepan with all of the stock ingredients, including the reserved skin and parsley stalks. Bring to the boil and simmer gently for 30 minutes, then strain through a fine-meshed sieve into a clean saucepan.

2 Add the skate fillets, cover with a piece of greaseproof paper, bring back to the boil and simmer for 3–4 minutes. Stir in the parsley and leave to infuse off the heat for 5 minutes.

3 Pour the skate and liquid into a fine-meshed sieve over a bowl. Return the strained liquid to a pan and simmer until it has been reduced by half.

4 Soak the gelatine leaf in cold water for a few minutes until it softens, then squeeze out as much water from it as you can and stir the leaf into the stock until it dissolves. Season the stock with salt and pepper to taste, then leave to cool.

5 Meanwhile, flake the skate into pieces (not too small) in a bowl with the parsley. When the stock is cool, stir it into the skate pieces and transfer to a serving dish or moulds. Leave to set in a cool place.

6 Make the pickled cucumber, if you like, by mixing all the ingredients and allow to stand for 30–60 minutes.

7 To serve, arrange the salad leaves on plates. Turn the skate out by dipping the container(s) in hot water first for a few seconds and then leave whole if in individual moulds, or cut in slices or simply spoon it out on top of the leaves. Spoon around some of the pickled cucumber if you have made it.

SERVES 4

800g–1kg skate, skinned and
   filleted, reserving the bones
   and skin for the stock
4 tbsp chopped parsley, reserving
   the stalks for the stock
1 (4g) gelatine leaf
salt and freshly ground white
   pepper
200g mixed small salad leaves

for the stock
3 shallots, chopped
1 small leek, roughly chopped and
   rinsed
1 tsp fennel seeds
1 bay leaf
10 white peppercorns
4 tbsp vermouth
1 litre fish stock (page 52, or a
   good-quality fish stock cube
   dissolved in that amount of hot
   water)

for the pickled cucumber (optional)
1 medium cucumber, cut into
   3mm dice
1 tbsp good-quality white wine
   vinegar
2 tbsp extra-virgin olive oil
2 tbsp chopped dill

OTHER SUITABLE FISH: eel, huss

Fillet of sea trout with mousserons

SERVES 4

4 sea trout fillets, each 160–180g,
    with the skin, scaled, and any
    residual bones removed
salt and freshly ground black
    pepper
vegetable oil, for frying
flour, for dusting (optional)
2 tbsp olive oil
3 large shallots, finely chopped
40g streaky bacon or pancetta,
    finely diced
125g mousserons or chanterelles
50g butter
2 tbsp chopped parsley

Sometimes also called salmon trout, sea trout has a texture that is slightly more delicate than that of salmon, but it can be used in much the same way. As with salmon, the flavour of wild and farmed fish can vary somewhat. The sea trout you find in the shops tends only to be wild and is difficult to distinguish from salmon, although I have seen a few farmed versions at the markets. The flavour is slightly earthy and delicate, and it doesn't take much cooking. It is actually the same fish as brown (river) trout but at a later stage in its life. After its juvenile stage inland, it migrates to the sea and develops a silvery sheen and saltwater metabolism. These beautiful fish vary widely in size. Mousserons are a tiny version of the St George's mushroom and have a delicate but earthy flavour to match the trout; if you can't find them, then chanterelles would be a good substitute.

1 Season the fish with salt and pepper. Heat the vegetable oil in a large frying pan, preferably non-stick (otherwise lightly flour the skin of the fish) and gently cook the fish portions, skin side first, over a medium heat for 3–4 minutes on each side, keeping them slightly pink in the middle and crisping the skin a little.

2 Meanwhile, heat the olive oil in another pan and gently cook the shallots and bacon in it for 3–4 minutes without allowing them to colour. Add the mushrooms and butter, lightly season with salt and pepper and continue to cook over a low heat for another 3–4 minutes until the mushrooms have softened.

3 Add the parsley, heat through for a minute, then spoon the mixture on to warmed plates and serve the sea trout portions on top.

OTHER SUITABLE FISH: Arctic char, large brown trout, large rainbow trout, salmon

Gravadlax

This delicious herb-cured salmon makes perfect party food and you can prepare it up to a week ahead. It also makes a good dinner party starter and you can just serve it on rye bread as open sandwiches. In fact, you can treat it in almost exactly the same way as you would smoked salmon, except I wouldn't recommend it with scrambled eggs (page 17). You may find it tricky getting your hands on the Swedish mustard – it's sweeter and without the kick that other mustards have. The obvious place, Ikea, no longer stocks it. You could use French's American mustard or just stick to Dijon. If you use all Dijon for the sauce, increase the sugar quantity to 2 tablespoons.

1 Lay the salmon fillet on a piece of cling film large enough to wrap back over the fish. Mix the sugar, salt, pepper and lime zest together, cover the fish with the mixture and leave at room temperature for 45 minutes.

2 Wrap the cling film over the fish so it's well sealed – use more if you need to. Place the fish on a tray and refrigerate for 36 hours.

3 Unwrap the salmon and discard any liquid that has formed, then lay the fish on a fresh piece of cling film. Sprinkle half the dill on the salmon then spread on the mustard and finally the rest of the dill. Wrap up tightly in the cling film and store in the fridge for 2-3 days before using.

4 To make the dill mustard sauce: whisk together the two mustards and the sugar, and then slowly add the vegetable oil, adjusting with a little warm water if the mixture becomes too thick. Add the dill and season with salt and freshly ground black pepper to taste.

5 To serve, remove the cling film and, using a long sharp carving knife, cut slices about 5mm thick at a 20-degree angle, turning the knife when you get to the skin. Serve about 4 slices per person, or more if you wish, with some of the dill mustard sauce.

SERVES 6-8 AS A STARTER

1 skin-on side of salmon, weighing about 1kg, trimmed and any pin-bones removed
85g brown, soft light brown or Demerara sugar
65g table or fine sea salt
1/2 tsp ground white pepper
finely grated zest of 1 lime
75g chopped fresh dill
75g Swedish mustard

for the dill mustard sauce
1 tsp Dijon mustard
125g Swedish mustard (see left)
2 tsp Demerara sugar
100ml vegetable oil
a little warm water (optional)
1 tbsp chopped dill
salt and freshly ground black pepper

OTHER SUITABLE FISH: sea trout, any firm-fleshed white fish

Red mullet & samphire salad with tomato vinaigrette

SERVES 4

150g samphire, trimmed

a little olive oil, for frying

4 red mullet fillets, each about 115g, any residual bones removed, and fillets halved

60g small salad leaves, such as purslane, baby spinach, corn salad

for the tomato vinaigrette

1 tbsp tarragon vinegar

1 small tomato, skinned and deseeded

4 tbsp olive oil

salt and freshly ground black pepper

Red mullet has a rich, almost gamy flavour, hence one of the French terms for it, *bécasse de mer* (woodcock of the sea). It is a beautiful-looking fish and normally has a price tag to match. It should be cooked and garnished simply.

1 Heat a large pan of water to blanch the samphire. Make the dressing: blend the vinegar, tomato and olive oil with 1 tablespoon of water until smooth. Strain and season with salt and pepper.

2 Heat a little olive oil in a non-stick frying pan over medium heat. Season the red mullet fillets with salt and pepper and fry them, skin side down first, for 1¹/₂ minutes on each side.

3 Meanwhile, blanch the samphire in the boiling water for 30 seconds only, then drain in a colander.

4 Dress the salad leaves with the dressing, lightly season with salt and pepper, and arrange on plates with the samphire and red mullet.

OTHER SUITABLE FISH: grey mullet, gurnard, sea bass, sea bream, snapper

Salade niçoise

SERVES 4

1 garlic clove, peeled

150g (podded weight) young
broad beans or French beans,
cooked until just tender

4 ripe plum tomatoes, skinned

2 spring onions, thinly sliced

12 good-quality canned anchovies
in olive oil, drained

24 small niçoise olives

salt and freshly ground black
pepper

6 tbsp extra-virgin olive oil

1 tbsp tarragon vinegar

300g good-quality canned or
freshly cooked tuna (see right)

2 soft-boiled eggs, shelled

8–10 basil leaves, torn in half

This is another of those 'classic' dishes that arrives on the plate in lots of different guises. All too often it is a garbage bin of ingredients put together with little care or thought, when it should just consist of some simple seasonal produce, well seasoned and dressed in style. It can be made as luxurious or as simple as you like, but it must reflect the food of the south. French beans are now commonly used, as are tiny artichokes. The tuna can be good-quality canned or, if you fancy cooking your own, fresh – preferably *ventrèche* or *ventresca*, the fatty belly – done slowly in some olive oil and herbs.

1 Rub the inside of a large bowl with the garlic. Add the beans, quartered tomatoes, onions, anchovies (whole or halved) and olives. Season with salt and pepper, add two-thirds each of the oil and vinegar, and mix well.

2 Add the tuna and halved eggs and gently mix in, trying not to break them up. Spoon over the remaining oil and vinegar. Scatter with the basil.

OTHER SUITABLE FISH: *marlin, salmon, swordfish*

Rare seared tuna with shaved fennel salad

The tuna must be as fresh as possible. It should be bright red and not look dull or discoloured, as this means that the blood has oxidized and it can then taste rather bitter.

1 Rub a heavy-based frying pan, preferably non-stick, with a little vegetable oil and heat until the oil is almost smoking. Meanwhile, season the tuna with salt and pepper, and sear it for about 30 seconds on all sides until lightly coloured, then refrigerate until required.

2 If the fennel's outer leaves are fibrous, peel them. Quarter the bulbs and cut out the cores. With a mandolin grater or very sharp knife, slice the fennel as thinly as possible and put in a bowl. Mix in some of the reserved tops, if you have any, the fennel seeds, vinegar and half the oil. Season, mix well and let stand for an hour.

3 Slice the tuna thinly and arrange on beds of the shaved fennel. Mix the chopped tomatoes with the remaining oil and spoon around as a garnish.

SERVES 4 AS A STARTER
vegetable oil, for frying
400g good-quality, very fresh
    tuna
salt and freshly ground white
    pepper
2 small fennel bulbs, any feathery
    tops reserved and finely chopped
10 fennel seeds, crushed
2 tbsp Chardonnay vinegar or
    2 tbsp good-quality white wine
    vinegar mixed with 1 tsp caster
    sugar
2 tbsp olive oil
2 skinned tomatoes, deseeded
    and diced, to garnish

OTHER SUITABLE FISH: marlin, salmon, swordfish

4 comfort*fish*

Kedgeree

The Hindi rice, lentil and onion dish of *khichri* has come a long way. The breakfast dish with which we are so familiar today was developed from that peasant meal by the British in India as a good way of using up fish and rice.

Smoked Finnan haddock makes the best kedgeree by far. The smokiness travels deliciously through the sauce and rice. Don't be tempted to buy bright yellow, dyed haddock fillet: no smoke on this earth has ever been known to produce that colour. A few prawns make a luxurious addition.

1 First, make the sauce: melt the butter in a heavy-based pan and gently cook the onion, garlic and ginger without allowing them to colour. Add all the spices and cook for another minute to release the flavours. Add the fish stock, bring to the boil and allow to reduce by half. Pour in the cream and simmer gently for 15 minutes. Blend the sauce in a liquidizer until smooth, then strain through a fine-meshed sieve. Adjust the seasoning.

2 Cook the rice in plenty of boiling, salted water for about 12-15 minutes, until it is just tender. Briefly drain in a colander and return to a pan off the heat with a lid on. This allows the rice to steam dry and gives it a fluffy, light texture.

3 To serve the kedgeree: reheat the curry sauce and add the cooked smoked haddock, salmon and coriander. Put the rice into a bowl, spoon over the fish and sauce, then scatter over the eggs. Serve with lime or lemon wedges.

SERVES 4

150g basmati rice, well rinsed

200g natural smoked haddock fillet, any residual bones removed and fillet lightly poached

150g salmon fillet, skinned, any residual bones removed and fillet lightly poached

3 eggs, hard-boiled, shelled and chopped

lime or lemon wedges, to serve

for the curry sauce

30g butter

1 large onion, finely chopped

1 garlic clove, crushed

2 tsp finely chopped root ginger

1/2 tsp ground turmeric

1/2 tsp ground cumin

1/2 tsp curry powder

1/2 tsp fenugreek seeds, crushed

good pinch of saffron threads

100ml fish stock (page 52, or 1/4 of a good-quality fish stock cube dissolved in that amount of hot water)

200ml double cream

salt and freshly ground black pepper

2 tbsp chopped coriander

OTHER SUITABLE FISH: any smoked white fish or a mixture of smoked and fresh, including salmon

Fish curry

SERVES 4

600g firm-fleshed fish fillet
    (snapper, pomfret, huss, etc.),
    any residual bones removed
    and fillets cut into 3–4cm
    chunks
salt and freshly ground white
    pepper
flour, for dusting
60g clarified butter or ghee
3 onions, roughly chopped
4 large garlic cloves, crushed
1–2 tbsp chopped root ginger
1 small medium-strength chilli,
    deseeded and finely chopped
1–2 tsp cumin seeds
1–2 tsp fenugreek seeds
1 tsp ground cumin
1 tsp ground turmeric
pinch of saffron strands
1 tsp curry powder
good pinch of curry leaves
1–2 tsp paprika
1–2 tsp fennel seeds
1–2 tsp mustard seeds
2 tsp tomato purée
1 lemon, halved
4 tbsp split yellow lentils
    (mung dhal), soaked in cold
    water for 1 hour
1.3 litres fish stock (page 52,
    or a good-quality fish stock
    cube dissolved in that amount
    of hot water)
2 tbsp chopped coriander leaves
100g coconut cream (block or liquid)
basmati rice, to serve

When I worked at the Dorchester Hotel in Park Lane we had a lovable bunch of Bangladeshi kitchen porters. Every day they'd make themselves a different curry for their staff meal. They would ask us to take them to the dry stores, where they'd mix their own spices, and we'd then give them chicken, meat, fish or vegetables.

They weren't interested in Dover sole or luxury fish and their favourite piece of fish was the head, which they added to a delicious curry that I remember to this day. Normally they'd use salmon heads, which would be cut into pieces, washed and put into the pot to sit on the highest heat in the middle of the stove with lots of ghee (clarified butter), onions, garlic and spices. They boiled the hell out of it for about an hour and the end result was fantastic. I often skipped kitchen-staff food in favour of the porters' curry.

If there's an Asian supermarket near you, look in the freezer and you'll find lots of unrecognizable fish, like boal and pomfret, native to the Indian Ocean and often firm-fleshed so well suited to curry.

1 Season the pieces of fish with salt and pepper and lightly flour them. Heat half the clarified butter or ghee in a large, heavy-based pan and fry the fish over a high heat until lightly coloured. Remove the fish with a slotted spoon and set aside.

2 Add the rest of the clarified butter or ghee to the pan and fry the onions, garlic, ginger and chilli for a few minutes until they begin to soften. Add all the spices and continue cooking for a couple of minutes to release the flavours, stirring every so often. Add the tomato purée, lemon halves, drained lentils and stock, bring to the boil, season with salt and pepper, and simmer gently for 1 hour.

3 After 1 hour, the lentils should have almost disintegrated, thickening the sauce; if not, simmer for another 15 minutes or so. Take a cupful of the sauce from the pan and blend in a liquidizer until smooth, then pour it back into the sauce.

4 Add the pieces of fish to the sauce and simmer for 10 minutes. Add the coriander and coconut cream, and simmer for 5 minutes more. Adjust the seasoning, if necessary. Serve with boiled basmati rice.

OTHER SUITABLE FISH: any firm white fish or shellfish

Brandade

Salt cod – *bacalao* to the Spanish, *baccalà* In Italy and *morue* in France – lends Itself to lots of different cooking methods. This is the French version, where the fish is cooked and puréed with potato and lots of garlic.

Traditional salt cod is split like a big kipper and salted, which means you end up with loads of fiddly bones. Instead, if you can get a hold of any, try to buy salted cod loins, which are nicely trimmed with no bones and skin. I've allowed for the trimmed loin here, so double the weight if you are using traditional salt cod. A couple of days before you need to cook it, soak the fish in plenty of cold water and change the water 3 or 4 times over 48 hours.

1 Soak the salt cod thoroughly as described above and, if using the traditional type, remove any fins and visible bones with a sharp knife.

2 Drain and put the fish in a pan with milk to cover, bring to the boil and simmer over a low heat for 25-30 minutes, then remove with a slotted spoon and transfer to a plate.

3 Preheat the oven to 180°C/gas 4. Put the onion and potatoes into the milk and return to the heat. Simmer until the potatoes are almost cooked, then add the garlic and simmer until the potatoes are fully cooked. Drain in a colander over a bowl, reserving the liquid.

4 Carefully flake the fish flesh off the bone, discarding any small bones. In a food processor, blend half the cod with a little of the reserved milk and the potato mixture. Transfer to a bowl and add the rest of the pieces of cod and the cream. Season with salt and pepper and mix well.

5 Put the mixture into individual ovenproof serving dishes (those little terracotta tapas/crema catalana dishes work well) or one large one. Mix the Parmesan, breadcrumbs and butter together, scatter over the top and bake for 35-40 minutes until lightly coloured.

SERVES 4 AS A STARTER
300-350g salt cod, soaked
  (see left)
milk, for poaching
1 onion, chopped
250g floury potatoes, cut into
  chunks
8 garlic cloves, roughly crushed
100ml double cream
salt and freshly ground white
  pepper
60g freshly grated Parmesan
  cheese
20g fresh white breadcrumbs
30g butter, melted

OTHER SUITABLE FISH: any salt fish, including home-salted

Fishcakes

SERVES 4

325g skinless fillets of white fish,
    any residual bones removed

salt and freshly ground white
    pepper

325g potato, peeled, cooked and
    mashed (but without added
    milk or butter)

1/2 tbsp anchovy essence

1/2 tbsp English mustard

2 tbsp chopped dill

flour, for dusting

vegetable oil, for frying

parsley sauce, to serve (page 28)

Fishcakes are a great way of using up offcuts and cheaper types of flaky fish that don't normally get used for frying and grilling, like whiting, coley etc. A bit of smoked haddock or cod in the mix always gives an added boost to the flavour, salmon imparts a good colour and can be used alone (adding a little tomato ketchup to the mix for a good colour), and a few dashes of anchovy essence are good additional seasoning.

1 Poach the fish gently in salted water for 3–4 minutes (or fish stock if you want to use it to make a sauce), drain, allow to cool and then flake the flesh.

2 Mix together the potato, half the fish, the anchovy essence, mustard, dill and salt and pepper until well amalgamated, then gently fold in the remaining fish. Mould the mixture into 4 large round cakes about 3cm thick or 8 smaller ones and refrigerate for about 1 hour.

3 Lightly flour the chilled fishcakes, shaking off any excess, and fry them in the vegetable oil for about 3–4 minutes on each side, until golden brown.

4 Serve the fishcakes with the parsley sauce.

Variations   There are lots of ways of varying the basic mix: you can use all smoked fish for a fine strong flavour; make Bajun fishcakes by using salt fish and chopped chilli, and breadcrumbing them; or make Thai fishcakes by using minced raw fish, omitting the potato and adding chopped chilli and galangal, chopped inner leaves of lemon grass and Thai fish sauce. For a very posh take on the theme, use langoustine or lobster and serve with sauce nantua (pages 102–3). You can also make mini versions of any of these types of fishcake to serve with drinks.

OTHER SUITABLE FISH: a wide range of fresh, smoked and salt fish, and shellfish

Deep-frying fish   Although I shouldn't admit to it, some of my most favourite

fried fish experiences have been had in Spain, where tiny young fish like hake, red mullet and eels are deep-fried whole, heads and all. It is actually illegal to land such young fish in the UK, but in other European nations they are considered unfit to be returned to the sea, as they won't survive, so are sold to restaurants and tapas bars for frying. Of course, we do have here the tradition of whitebait, the fry of herrings or sprats – which are legal – simply floured and deep-fried, then sprinkled with cayenne and served with lemon wedges.

Most fish fillets and shellfish can be cut up into goujon-like pieces and deep-fried to make excellent nibbles when you arrive at the table, simply served with lemon wedges. In Japan you will get them served as tempura and in Spain as *pescaditos fritos*, which always makes me laugh, as it sounds like a Gypsy Kings' song.

Fish really suits being deep-fried within a protective coating like a batter, as the high temperature of the oil cooks the fish rapidly and the coating protects the delicate flesh and also seals in all the flavour and natural moisture.

Deep-frying, perhaps surprisingly, done correctly is not such an unhealthy way to cook, as the food

absorbs very little oil. It also tastes delicious and has that wonderful texture contrast of the crisp coating and the succulent tender fish inside. To deep-fry correctly you must have plenty of oil and it must be at the right temperature – and stay at that temperature. As keeping the oil temperature steady is so important, it is obviously not a good idea to add too much food to the hot oil at a time, so deep-frying is usually best done in smallish batches.

As a general rule the oil temperature should be at least 160ºC and up to 180–190ºC. (Many cookbooks will tell you that a cube of stale bread thrown into oil at the right temperature will brown in 60 seconds.) This is considerably hotter than boiling water, and is obviously potentially hazardous if you are careless. Remember, if you are not using an automatic deep-fryer, never leave heating oil unattended as it will spontaneously ignite if allowed to get too hot – in other words, beyond its smoking point.

After frying the fish, drain it on kitchen paper to soak up excess oil, season with salt and keep warm – but don't cover it or the crisp coating will go soggy. A medium oven with the door open is a good answer.

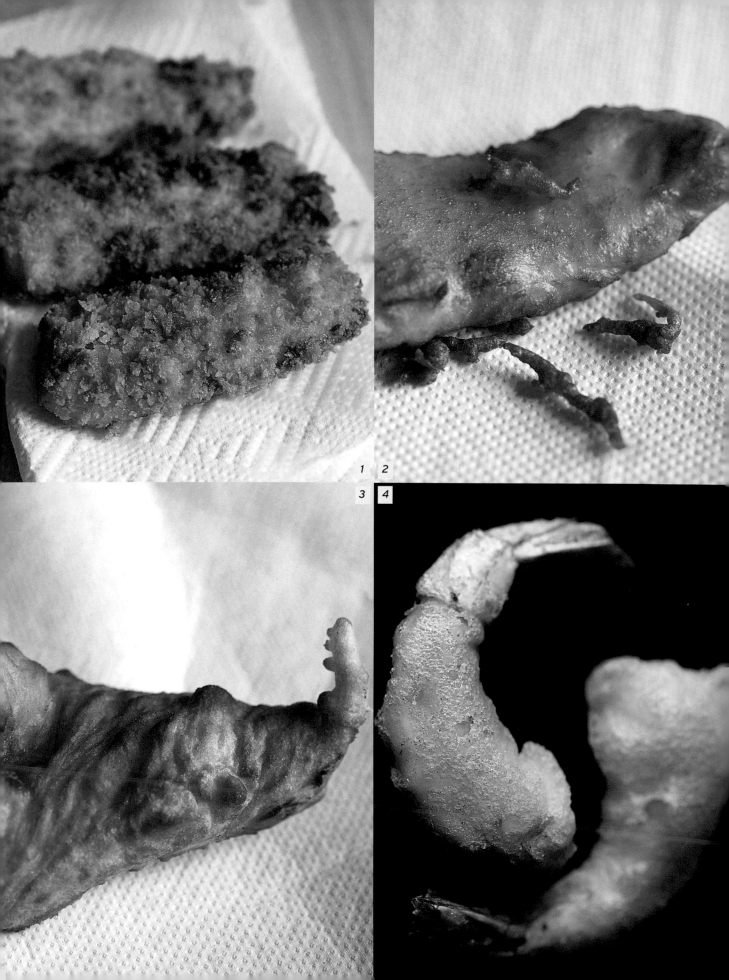

Egg and breadcrumb coating (1) is a more usual treatment for less firm fish, like plaice. The fish must first be patted quite dry then seasoned with salt and pepper and dusted with flour, the excess patted off. It is then dipped in beaten egg and finally in fresh white breadcrumbs. This can be varied by adding some grated Parmesan or herbs to the crumbs.

Batter coating Fish to be coated in batter should also first be coated in flour or cornflour and any excess patted off.

For a *yeast batter (2)*, which gives a nice thick coating that holds up well when cooked: in a small bowl, dissolve 4g easy-blend yeast in a little milk and leave in a warm place for about 10 minutes. In a larger bowl, mix 250ml milk, 1 small egg yolk, 75g plain flour, 75g cornflour, a pinch of cayenne pepper and 1/4 teaspoon baking powder into a batter, add the yeast mixture and season to taste with salt. Cover and leave at room temperature for 1 1/2–2 hours, until it begins to ferment. If the batter seems too thick, add a little more milk or water.

For a light and tasty traditional *'chippie' beer batter (3)* that goes well with fish: simply sift 250g flour into 250ml light beer, mix well and season to taste. An added spoonful of olive oil adds sheen and crispness.

For a light, crisp *tempura batter (4):* quickly whisk 200ml iced water with 50g plain flour and 50g potato flour with a little salt to taste until well combined; don't worry if there are any lumps in it (if it is too smooth, it will be tough when cooked).

Accompaniments for deep-fried fish: To make *tartare sauce* for 4: finely chop 25g gherkins, and rinse and finely chop 25g capers. Mix these with 1/2 tablespoon chopped parsley and 4 tablespoons mayonnaise (see page 62). Season to taste with lemon juice and salt and freshly ground black pepper.

To make a *minted pea purée* for 6–8: heat 25g butter in a pan and cook 1 large shallot, finely chopped, gently in it until soft. Add 400g frozen peas, 100ml vegetable stock and 6–8 mint leaves. Season and simmer for 10–12 minutes. Coarsely blend in a food processor, then adjust the seasoning.

Haddock specials

SERVES 4

2 large baking potatoes

salt and freshly ground white
    pepper

150g haddock fillets,
    skinned and any residual bones
    removed

vegetable or corn oil, for deep-
    frying

flour, for dusting

yeast batter (page 83)

minted pea purée (page 83)
    and/or tartare sauce
    (page 83), to serve

These totally delicious treats take me right back to childhood.
I loved simple potato fritters done in this way, but with the
succulent flakes of white fish sandwiched between them they are
just sublime. You can make mini versions of these to serve as
canapés with drinks.

1 Cook the baking potatoes in their skins in boiling salted water for
25 minutes and leave to cool.

2 Remove the skins from the potatoes and slice them into sixteen 1cm
discs. Cut the haddock into pieces big enough to fit on top of 8 of the
potato slices, season and sandwich them with another slice of potato,
pressing firmly.

3 Meanwhile, heat the oil in a deep-fat fryer or heavy-bottomed pan
(half full) to 160ºC. Season the potato sandwiches and lightly flour
them, then dip them in batter, allowing excess to drip off, and fry them
for about 4–5 minutes until golden. Remove them with a slotted spoon
and transfer them to some kitchen paper to drain.

4 Serve with minted pea purée and/or tartare sauce.

OTHER SUITABLE FISH: any white fish, such as baramundi, coley, whiting, or flat fish like brill, dab, plaice or sole

Smoked haddock with poached egg & colcannon

illustrated on previous page

SERVES 4

about 400ml milk, for poaching

200ml fish stock (page 52 or ½
good-quality fish stock cube
dissolved in that amount of hot
water)

1 bay leaf

4 skinned smoked haddock
portions, each about 160g, any
residual bones removed

2 shallots, finely chopped

300ml double cream

1 tbsp chopped dill

4 eggs

knob of butter

for the colcannon

300g Savoy cabbage, cut into
rough 2cm pieces

salt and freshly ground white
pepper

6 spring onions, shredded

400g floury potatoes, cooked and
mashed

40g butter, or more if necessary

This is a classic way to serve smoked haddock, but with my own little twist. There is nothing quite like that bursting egg yolk running into the velvety colcannon – the Irish cabbage-packed mashed potato – and the combination of all the ingredients just falling into place.

1 First make the colcannon: cook the cabbage in boiling salted water for about 5–6 minutes until soft, but not overcooked. Add the spring onions and simmer for another 30 seconds, drain in a colander, then mix with the mashed potato and butter and season again with salt and pepper. Keep warm in a covered pan until required, or allow to cool down and then reheat in the microwave cooker when required.

2 While the colcannon is cooking, bring the milk and fish stock to the boil with the bay leaf. Add the smoked haddock, bring back to the boil and simmer gently for 3–4 minutes. Remove the fish carefully with a slotted spoon and transfer to a warmed plate. Cover with foil and keep warm (over the potatoes would be good).

3 Transfer half of the cooking liquid to a clean pan, add the shallots and boil to reduce the liquid by two-thirds. Add the double cream and reduce it again by two-thirds, or until it thickens to coating consistency. Adjust the seasoning, if necessary, add the chopped dill and simmer for another minute.

4 While the liquid is being reduced, poach the eggs until just set but still soft inside.

5 Spoon the colcannon on to warmed plates, carefully break the haddock fillets in half and press gently into the colcannon. Drain the eggs with a slotted spoon and rest them in between the two pieces of haddock. Finish the sauce by stirring in the knob of butter and spoon it over the eggs and fish to serve.

OTHER SUITABLE FISH: any smoked white fish

Fish fingers

Making these yourself is a bit more labour-intensive than reaching into the freezer for a pack, but the flavour makes it well worth the extra effort. We know that kids love them, and grown-ups too. You can use any type of firm or semi-firm white fish from haddock and cod to hoki and pollack – even salmon works well.

1 Season the pieces of fish. Spread the flour in a shallow dish, put the beaten egg in another and the breadcrumbs in a third. Coat the pieces of fish first in the flour, then in the egg and finally in the breadcrumbs.

2 Heat a generous amount of oil in a heavy frying pan and cook the fish fingers for about 2 minutes on each side, until nicely browned. Drain on kitchen paper and serve with some minted pea purée and/or tartare sauce.

SERVES 4

500g skinless fish fillet, any residual bones removed and fillets cut into 8 pieces about 2x8cm, depending on the width of the fillets

salt and freshly ground white pepper

flour, for coating

1 large egg, beaten

100g fresh white breadcrumbs

vegetable or corn oil, for frying

minted pea purée (page 83) and/or tartare sauce (page 83), to serve

OTHER SUITABLE FISH: any firm or semi-firm white fish, salmon

Herring salad

SERVES 4

100g soft herring roes

salt and freshly ground white
   pepper

good knob of butter

80g fine curly endive

125g smoked or cured herring
   fillet, cut into 2cm pieces

for the dressing

1 tbsp good-quality tarragon
   vinegar

2 tsp Dijon mustard

1 garlic clove, peeled

2 tbsp olive oil

2 tbsp vegetable or corn oil

a few sprigs of tarragon

salt and freshly ground black
   pepper

for the herring roe pâté

125g butter, softened

125g soft herring roes

salt and cayenne pepper

1 tbsp double cream

juice of ½ lemon

We generally eat herring roes fried and served on hot buttered toast. Like chicken livers and other offal, they lend themselves to lots of other preparations and dishes. If you can have a chicken liver salad, why not do the same with herring roes and serve the fillets too.

1 First make the dressing: put all of the ingredients in a clean bottle or jar, give them a good shake and leave to infuse at room temperature, preferably overnight.

2 A few hours ahead, make the herring roe pâté: melt 30g of the butter in a frying pan, season the roes with salt and cayenne pepper, and gently sauté them over a medium heat for 3-4 minutes. Add the rest of the butter to the pan until it's just melted, then transfer to a food processor, add the cream and blend until smooth. Season with more salt and cayenne pepper to taste and add the lemon juice. Transfer to a bowl and chill for a couple of hours.

3 Season the other soft roes with salt and white pepper and fry in the butter over a medium heat for 4-5 minutes until nicely coloured.

4 To serve, dress the curly endive with the dressing and arrange on plates. Spoon the pâté neatly on the salad and arrange the warm roes and pieces of smoked herring fillet on the leaves.

Variations   There are several ways of enlivening the flavour of the herring roe pâté: you could add some chopped dill, a tablespoon or two of freshly grated horseradish or a small handful of chopped capers. Alternatively, try spiking it with a dash of pastis or Ricard.

OTHER SUITABLE FISH: monkfish, using the liver as well as the fillet or cheeks

Eels in green sauce

Eels have a particular following; in this country their aficionados are especially found in the East End of London, where you still occasionally see 'eel and pie' shops and fish stands selling bowls of jellied eels. Eels can have a rather earthy flavour, depending on where they have been living and feeding, so try to find the source when you are buying. Medium-to-small eels up to 1.5 kilos are the perfect size for cooking. As it is a real palaver, get your fishmonger to do the skinning and cleaning. Eels in green sauce is quite a classic dish in Europe, though you don't see it on many menus. I enjoyed a really good version in an old brasserie in Brussels which prompted me to experiment with it when I got back home.

1 Cut the eels into 3-4cm pieces and rinse well. Put them in a pan with the fish stock, shallots, bay leaf, white wine and vermouth, and season with salt and pepper. Bring to the boil and poach for 10-15 minutes. Remove the eels from the cooking liquor with a slotted spoon and set aside.

2 Reduce the cooking liquor down by two-thirds, then add the double cream. Bring back to the boil and simmer until it has reduced by about half again and has thickened.

3 Add the watercress, parsley and chervil, and simmer for 3 minutes. Blend the sauce in a liquidizer until smooth, then strain through a fine-meshed sieve into a clean pan. The sauce should be a thick coating consistency; if not, simmer it for a few minutes until it thickens.

4 Adjust the seasoning, if necessary, and add the butter and eels. Simmer for 2-3 minutes to reheat and serve with mash or boiled potatoes.

SERVES 4

1.5-2kg live eels, skinned, cleaned and heads removed
1 litre fish stock (page 52 or a good-quality fish stock cube dissolved in that amount of hot water)
4 shallots, roughly chopped
1 bay leaf
3 tbsp white wine
3 tbsp vermouth
salt and freshly ground white pepper
400ml double cream
100g watercress, any thick stalks removed
30g parsley, large stalks removed
15g chervil, large stalks removed
good knob of butter

OTHER SUITABLE FISH: huss, monkfish

Scallops with black pudding, girolles & mousseline potato

The idea of scallops and black pudding may seem a bit weird, but lots of shellfish marry perfectly with meat, like the classic pairing of oysters with spicy sausage. The quality of the black pudding is quite important here – I wouldn't want to be serving delicate fresh scallops with that cheap black pudding that tastes of sawdust. I favour *morcilla*, the Spanish black pudding, for this dish, which is somewhere between the sometimes-too-soft French *boudin noir* and those from the North of England and Scotland. Nothing is wrong with any of these, it's just that the texture needs to be correct to complement the whole dish. Also try to buy black pudding that is about 2–3cm in diameter, a similar size to the scallops, or you will have to quarter the large puddings.

1 Melt 80g of the butter in a frying pan until it begins to foam, but don't let it brown. Add the garlic and girolles, season with salt and pepper and cook gently for 2–3 minutes until these begin to soften. Add the parsley and remove from the heat.

2 Meanwhile, lightly oil a non-stick frying pan or a trusty cast-iron one and heat it over a medium-to-high flame. Season the scallops with salt and pepper and cook for a minute on each side. Remove from the pan and keep warm, then cook the black pudding for about a minute again on each side.

3 Meanwhile, heat the mashed potato through, remove from the heat, stir in the remaining butter and the cream, and season. The potato should be of a thick sauce-like consistency and spoonable.

4 To serve, spoon the potato flat on warmed plates, arrange the scallops and black pudding alternating on the potato and spoon over the girolles and butter.

SERVES 4

120g butter
1 small garlic clove, crushed
125g small girolle mushrooms, wiped
salt and freshly ground white pepper
1 tbsp chopped parsley
olive oil, for frying
12 medium-sized scallops, cut from the shell, briefly rinsed and patted dry on kitchen paper
12 slices of black pudding, each about 1cm thick
200g floury potato, peeled, cooked and mashed
3 tbsp double cream

OTHER SUITABLE FISH: langoustine, lobster, squid

Spiced baked spider crab

SERVES 4 AS A FIRST COURSE

1 large cooked spider crab or
   brown crab, about 1.5–2kg
200g extra brown crab meat
1/2 onion, finely chopped
1 garlic clove, crushed
10g knob of ginger, scraped and
   finely chopped
1/2 small mild chilli, deseeded
   and finely chopped
115ml olive oil
3 tbsp sherry
3 tbsp fish stock (page 52, or
   a corner of a good-quality fish
   stock cube dissolved in that
   amount of hot water)
50g fresh white breadcrumbs
juice of 1/2 lemon
salt and freshly ground black
   pepper
thin slices of toast, to serve

If only I had known what I was doing as a kid, throwing those ugly spider crabs out of my net and back into the water. My friend Nigel, who makes bespoke fishing nets, does a bit of part-time potting for crabs and also discriminates against the ugly ones. He is an old hand, though, and instead of throwing them back, he sells them to an export company which, in turn, sells them to Spain. Which is where, in fact, I came across a similar dish to this, at a fish restaurant in St Feliu de Guixols, near Palamos on the Costa Brava.

Spider crabs are hard to come by in this country as, like Nigel, we export most of them. They can be bought cooked, although you may need to order them in advance. To cook them yourself, plunge them into simmering salted water for about 15 minutes per kilo.

1 To get the meat out of the crab, twist the legs and claws off, then crack them open and remove the white meat. Now turn the main body on its back and twist off the pointed flap. Push the tip of a table knife between the main shell and the bit to which the legs were attached, and twist the blade to separate the two, then push it up and remove. Scoop out the brown meat in the well of the shell and put with the leg and claw meat. On the other part of the body, remove the 'dead man's fingers' (the feathery grey gills attached to the body) and discard. Split the body in half with a heavy knife. Now patiently pick out the white meat from the little cavities in the body. Add to the rest of the meat. Clean and reserve the shell if you want to use it for serving.

2 Gently cook the onion, garlic, ginger and chilli in 2 teaspoons of the oil until soft. Add the sherry, fish stock and brown crab meat (to boost the flavour), stir well then add most of the breadcrumbs (reserving a few to scatter on top), half the lemon juice and seasoning to taste. Bring just to the boil and simmer for 15 minutes, stirring occasionally.

3 Preheat a hot grill. In a blender, process one-third of the mix with the rest of the olive oil, then stir it back into the mixture along with the crab meat. Add more lemon juice and seasoning if necessary.

4 Spoon into the shell or an ovenproof serving dish and scatter over the reserved breadcrumbs. Lightly brown under the grill. Serve with toast.

OTHER SUITABLE FISH: brown crab

Prawn burgers

SERVES 4

550g raw seawater prawns,
   shelled and deveined

150g firm white fish, boned and
   skinned

1/2 bunch of spring onions, finely
   chopped

1 tsp Worcestershire sauce

3 tbsp mayonnaise

pinch of cayenne pepper

salt and freshly ground black
   pepper

fresh white breadcrumbs, to coat

vegetable oil, for deep-frying

4 burger buns, to serve

for the spiced tartare sauce

3 tbsp good-quality mayonnaise
   (page 62 or ready-made)

20g capers, chopped

20g gherkins, chopped

4-5 drops of Tabasco sauce

I saw this recipe in the American food magazine *Saveur* and I have used it several times since. It's important to use seawater prawns, as opposed to freshwater, as the taste is far superior.

1 Put the prawns and white fish in a food processor and blend to a coarse purée. Put this and all of the remaining ingredients except the breadcrumbs into a bowl, mix well and season with salt and pepper. Make a tiny burger shape with a little of the mix, dredge with some breadcrumbs and fry in a little oil to test the seasoning of the mix. Add more seasoning if necessary.

2 Divide the rest of the mix into 4 flat patties a little larger than the buns and chill for 30-40 minutes.

3 Meanwhile, make the spiced tartare sauce by mixing all of the ingredients together.

4 Preheat oil for deep-frying to 170°C. Dredge the burgers in breadcrumbs, pressing them into the burgers, and deep-fry for 4-5 minutes until golden.

5 Meanwhile, lightly toast the burger buns, spread them with a spoonful of the spiced tartare sauce and serve the burgers in them.

Variation For a novel way to consume a high-quality fish standing round the barbecue and chatting to friends, mince some fresh tuna, including a bit of the fatty belly, season, form it into patties and griddle until nicely coloured on the outside but rare on the inside, then serve in burger buns with some spiced tartare sauce or a mixture of 2 parts tomato ketchup to 1 part sweet American mustard.

OTHER SUITABLE FISH: firm-fleshed fish, such as grouper and snapper, and most shellfish, especially prawns

Fritto misto di mare

1 Preheat oil for deep-frying to 160–180°C and a warm oven. Season the flour well with salt and cayenne pepper and put into a dish. Put the milk into another dish and have a third one ready for the finished pieces. Pass the pieces of fish, etc., firstly through the flour, then through the milk and again through the flour, shaking off the excess each time and putting them into the third dish.

2 Fry a handful of the fish, etc., for 3–4 minutes only, until they are uniformly golden. Remove them from the oil with a slotted spoon and drain on some kitchen paper. Repeat with the rest of the fish, keeping the cooked fish, etc., hot in the warm oven until they are all cooked.

3 Serve with wedges of lemon.

SERVES 4 AS A STARTER
vegetable oil, for deep-frying
flour, for dusting
salt and cayenne pepper
milk, for coating
300g fish fillet, any residual
  bones removed and fillets cut
  into bite-sized pieces, or fish
  fry like whitebait
200g peeled raw prawns,
  deveined
200g squid rings
lemon wedges, to serve

OTHER SUITABLE FISH: most firm-fleshed fish, scallops

Fish pie

Fish pie is honest, down-to-earth food, packed with flavours. It makes perfect comfort food if you are sitting in front of the television after a hard day, but works equally well as a dinner party main course. You can make this dish the day before and keep it in the fridge overnight. The basic recipe can be varied endlessly, according to what fish are available and what you like, but it is always good to include some smoked fish. Other than salmon, though, it is usually best to avoid oily fish. The mashed potato topping also gives lots of scope for jazzing up: you can flavour it with more cheese, some herbs or even saffron for a touch of luxury.

1 In a large saucepan, bring the fish stock and vermouth to the boil, add the onion and fennel, and cook gently for 8 minutes. Add the fish and prawns, and poach gently for 2 minutes. Drain in a colander over a bowl, reserving the cooking liquid, and leave to cool.

2 To make the sauce: melt the butter in a heavy-based pan over a low heat, then stir in the flour and cook gently for a minute. Gradually add the reserved fish poaching liquid, stirring well until it has all been added and the mixture is smooth. Bring to the boil and simmer gently for 30 minutes. Add the cream and continue to simmer for 10 minutes or so until the sauce has a thick consistency. Stir in the mustard and anchovy essence. Season with salt and freshly ground white pepper if necessary, and leave to cool for about 15 minutes or so.

3 Gently fold into the sauce the cooked fish and prawns with the fennel and onion pieces, and the herbs. Spoon into a large pie dish or several individual ones, filling to 3cm from the top. Leave to set for about 30 minutes, so that the potato will sit on the sauce.

4 Meanwhile, preheat the oven to 180°C/gas 4 and mix the butter into the mashed potato. Season with a little salt and freshly ground white pepper and add a little milk so that it is just soft enough to pipe with a piping bag or simply spread with a spatula on to the pies.

5 Bake for 30 minutes (20 for little pies). Scatter on the breadcrumbs and cheese, and bake for 10-15 minutes more until golden on top.

SERVES 4-6

500 ml fish stock (page 52, or a good-quality fish stock cube dissolved in that amount of hot water)

2 tbsp dry vermouth

1 large onion, finely chopped

1 fennel bulb, cored and finely diced (optional)

250g fillets of white fish, such as pollack, skinned, any residual bones removed and fillets cut into rough 3cm chunks

175g salmon fillet, skinned, any residual bones removed and fillets cut into rough 3cm chunks

175g smoked fish fillet, skinned, any residual bones removed and fillets cut into rough 3cm chunks

150g small-to-medium peeled raw prawns (optional)

2 tbsp chopped mixed green herbs, such as parsley, dill and chervil

60g butter

1.5kg potatoes, cooked and mashed

a little milk

20g fresh white breadcrumbs

20g grated Parmesan cheese

for the sauce

50g butter

50g flour

175ml double cream

2 tsp Dijon mustard

1 tsp anchovy essence

salt and freshly ground white pepper

OTHER SUITABLE FISH: *any fish except game fish, like swordfish and tuna*

Paella

SERVES 4

500g chicken legs or rabbit
  hindquarters, chopped into
  pieces on the bone
salt and freshly ground black
  pepper
4 tbsp olive oil
1 large onion, finely chopped
4 garlic cloves, crushed
2 tsp roughly chopped fresh
  thyme
60g cooking chorizo sausage,
  thinly sliced
1 tsp saffron strands or ground
  saffron
1 tbsp tomato purée
200g paella or risotto rice
700ml chicken stock
700ml fish stock (page 52, or a
  good-quality fish stock cube
  dissolved in that amount of hot
  water)
16 pieces of langoustine or raw
  tiger prawns with the heads on
300g mussels, washed and
  debearded, discarding any that
  stay stubbornly open when
  tapped
150g fresh (shelled weight) or
  frozen peas, cooked in salted
  water with a little sugar
150g fresh (shelled weight) or
  frozen broad beans, cooked in
  salted water

This is a dish that is often misunderstood when copied, usually because the real thing has never been experienced. What should go into a paella? This depends a good deal on where you eat it. Depending on how much – and what type of – fish and/or meat goes into it, the colour will vary. The best paellas are often the most unattractively coloured ones in the most unusual places; I've had it with rabbit and snails in places that you can't reach by road. Certain restaurants in Spain will offer a range of different types, some of which are almost black due to the use of cuttlefish ink, usually containing what's available in the local market that day.

1 Preheat the oven to 200°C/gas 6. Season the chicken or rabbit with salt and pepper and roast with half of the olive oil poured over them for 30–40 minutes until nicely coloured.

2 In a large cast-iron frying pan (that will fit in your oven) or a paella pan, gently fry the onion, garlic, thyme and chorizo in the rest of the olive oil until soft.

3 Add the saffron, tomato purée and the rice, and stir well. Add half of each of the chicken and fish stocks with the chicken pieces (including any liquid from the pan), stir well and season with salt and pepper.

4 Cover with a lid and cook in the oven for 15 minutes, stirring a couple of times during cooking. Add the langoustine, mussels, peas and broad beans with half of the remaining stocks, stir well, cover and return to the oven for another 10 minutes or until the mussels have opened (one or two may not, so don't keep cooking just for them once most have opened, just discard the closed ones).

5 Remove from the oven. The paella should have quite a wet consistency; if not, add the rest of the stocks and stir on a low heat for a couple of minutes.

6 Serve in the cooking dish, if possible, for a fairly authentic paella, depending on where you've eaten on holiday.

OTHER SUITABLE FISH: clams, cockles, lobster, scallops

Chicken & crayfish pies

SERVES 4

24 crayfish tails

salt and freshly ground white
  pepper

500g boned and skinned chicken
  thighs, halved

a little cornflour (optional)

1 tbsp chopped parsley

1/2 tbsp chopped tarragon leaves

350–400g good-quality puff
  pastry, rolled out to 5mm thick

1 egg, beaten, to glaze

for the sauce nantua

4 shallots, roughly chopped

1 garlic clove, chopped

vegetable oil, for frying

Freshwater crayfish, or crawfish as they are known in Louisiana, can have very little flavour. However, using a rich creamy sauce nantua, made from their shells, gives this pie a real full shellfish flavour to go with the mellow taste of the chicken. You can replace the chicken thighs with breast, but I wouldn't recommend it as they tend to dry out. If you can't find any fresh crayfish, then use lobster or crawfish (rock lobster), or even some langoustines. Alternatively, you can buy precooked crayfish tails in brine and just make a double amount of sauce from the chicken stock.

1 To cook the crayfish: bring a large pan of well-salted water to the boil, add the crayfish and simmer for 3 minutes. Remove the crayfish and plunge them into cold water. Remove the meat from the shells and the claws if they are big enough and reserve. Break the shells up a little with a heavy knife and reserve for the sauce.

2 To make the sauce nantua: in a large heavy-based pan, fry the crayfish shells, shallots and garlic in a little oil over a medium heat for about 6-7 minutes, until they begin to colour lightly. Add the butter and flour and stir in well. Add the saffron, tarragon and tomato purée, and stir well. Gradually stir in the wine and stock, bring to the boil and simmer for about 10 minutes until reduced by roughly half. Add the cream, season lightly, bring to the boil and simmer gently for about 30 minutes until reduced by half and a good thick consistency.

3 Strain the sauce in a colander into a bowl and stir the shells with a spoon to ensure all the sauce goes through. Remove about 10 per cent of the shells (about half a cupful) and blend with the strained sauce in a liquidizer. Strain in a fine-meshed sieve.

4 Bring the sauce back to the boil and gently poach the chicken thighs in it for 5 minutes. Remove with a slotted spoon and set aside.

5 The sauce should be a thick coating consistency by now; if not, simmer a little longer or dilute a little cornflour in water and stir into the sauce. Leave to cool.

6 Mix the chicken, crayfish, parsley and tarragon into the thickened sauce. Adjust the seasoning if necessary, then fill 4 individual pie dishes, or one large one, with this mixture to about 1cm from the top.

7 Cut out tops or a top from the pastry for the pie(s) about 2cm larger all the way round than the dish(es). Brush the edges of the pastry with a little of the beaten egg. Lay the pastry on top, pressing the egg-washed side against the rim of the dish. Cut a small slit in the top of the pie(s) to allow steam to escape and brush with beaten egg. Leave to rest in a cool place for 30 minutes.

8 Preheat the oven to 200°C/ gas 6. Cook the pie(s) in the oven for 40-50 minutes, until the pastry is golden.

good knob of butter

1 tbsp flour

good pinch of saffron strands

a few sprigs of tarragon

1-2 tbsp tomato purée

4 tbsp white wine

300ml hot fish stock (page 52, or 1/2 good-quality fish stock cube dissolved in that amount of hot water)

350ml double cream

salt and freshly ground black pepper

OTHER SUITABLE FISH: langoustines, lobster, prawns

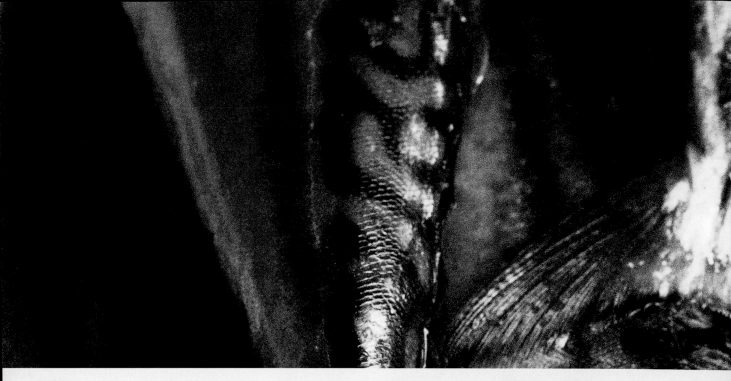

5 super-healthy*fish*

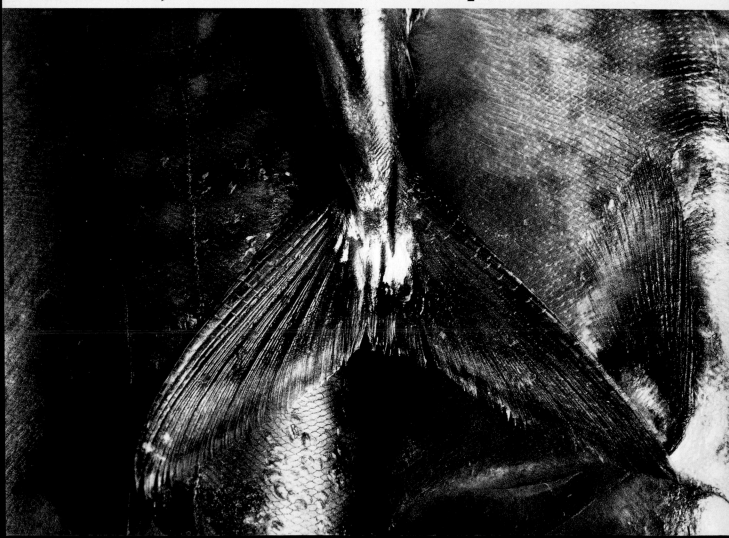

Seared mackerel with stir-fried Chinese greens

Mackerel really must be eaten within a couple of days of being caught, so check – I know it's a difficult one... and your fishmonger may get offended if you ask him if it's really fresh. I was spoilt as a kid, as we would catch them by the dozens off the local pier and end up using them for bait. When I did get round to eating them, the flavour was as good as you can get from fresh fish. Since then I have had very sensitive taste buds to these little scavengers of the sea.

The great thing about Chinese greens is that they are really tender, right down to the stalks. Most of the major supermarkets often stock several different types, with preparation and cooking instructions printed on the packaging. This method works with any of the varieties.

1 In a wok or heavy-based frying pan, heat 2 tablespoons of the sesame oil and gently fry the garlic, Szechuan pepper, ginger and spring onions until their aromas rise. Turn the heat up and add the greens, stirring continuously for about a minute. Add the soy sauce, stir well and keep warm while the mackerel is cooking.

2 Score the mackerel fillets 4 or 5 times across their width with a sharp knife. Season the fillets with salt and pepper, lightly flour them and pat off the excess with your hands.

3 Heat the remaining sesame oil and the vegetable oil in a non-stick frying pan and fry the fillets in this over a medium heat, skin side down first, for 2-3 minutes on each side.

4 Spoon the greens on to warmed plates and place the mackerel on top, skin side up.

SERVES 4

3 tbsp sesame oil

2 garlic cloves, crushed

1/2 tsp crushed Szechuan pepper

small piece of root ginger, peeled and shredded

4-5 spring onions, each cut at an angle into 4

500g Chinese greens, such as pak choi or similar, leaves removed from the root

1 tbsp light soy sauce

4 large mackerel fillets, each about 140–160g, or 8 smaller ones, any residual bones removed

salt and freshly ground black pepper

flour, for dusting

1 tbsp vegetable oil

OTHER SUITABLE FISH: most types of fish

Herrings with Alsacienne cabbage

SERVES 4

4 large herring fillets, each about
125–150g, or 8 smaller fillets,
scaled and cleaned, and any
residual bones removed

salt and freshly ground white
pepper

flour, for dusting

vegetable oil, for frying

for the Alsacienne cabbage

1 tbsp olive oil

1 onion, thinly sliced

4 juniper berries, crushed

1/2 tsp caraway seeds

1 small white cabbage, about
700g–1kg, shredded

good knob of butter (optional)

salt and freshly ground black
pepper

2 tbsp good-quality white wine
vinegar, like Chardonnay

250ml vegetable or chicken stock
(or 1/4 good-quality stock cube
dissolved in that amount of
hot water)

for the dressing

1 tbsp good-quality white wine
vinegar, like Chardonnay

1 tsp Dijon mustard

2 tsp grainy mustard

1/2 tsp caster sugar

2 tbsp corn oil

2 tbsp olive oil

1/2 tbsp chopped dill

Because herring is an oily fish, frying or grilling is probably the best way to cook it. If you've eaten fish choucroute, you will recognize this style of cabbage. It also suits oily fish like this perfectly, as it cuts the oiliness and makes it more digestible. If you're not too fussed about the dish actually being super-healthy, then add a few tablespoons of cream to the cabbage towards the end of cooking and continue simmering until the cabbage has absorbed all the cream.

1 First prepare the cabbage: heat the olive oil in a large heavy-based pan and gently cook the onion in it with the juniper berries and the caraway, covered, for a few minutes until the onion is soft. Add the cabbage and the butter, if using. Season with salt and freshly ground black pepper, and cook for another 5 minutes with the lid on, stirring occasionally. Add the vinegar and stock, turn the heat up a little and continue cooking for another 5 minutes, stirring occasionally, until the liquid has evaporated and the cabbage is softening. Cover with a lid and cook on a low heat for 15–20 minutes, stirring every so often, until the cabbage is tender. Should any liquid be left at this point, uncover and cook a little longer until it has gone. Adjust the seasoning, if necessary.

2 While the cabbage is cooking, make the dressing: mix the vinegar with the two mustards and sugar, then whisk in the oils. Season with salt and pepper and stir in the dill.

3 Season the herring fillets with salt and freshly ground white pepper, and lightly flour the skin side, patting off any excess with your hands. Heat a little vegetable oil in a non-stick frying pan and cook the herring fillets, skin side down first, for about 3 minutes on each side, getting the skin as crisp as possible without allowing it to burn.

4 To serve: spoon the cabbage on to the plates and arrange the herring fillets on top. Spoon the dressing around.

OTHER SUITABLE FISH: any oily fish

Grilled sardines with Essaouira salad

This is typical of the salad served on the quayside in Essaouira, on Morocco's Atlantic coast. It works really well with oily fish, like sardines or mackerel, as the acidity of the preserved lemon cuts the oiliness of the fish in a refreshingly tart way. You can buy preserved lemons in larger supermarkets. *Ras el hanout* is a rich and complex Moroccan spice mix that is slightly different wherever you buy it, but tends to feature ginger, cumin, anise, cinnamon, nutmeg, cloves, cardamom, mace and turmeric, together with crushed dried flowers like lavender and rose. Good delis and ethnic foods stores will sell versions of it.

1 Cut the peppers into 4 lengthways, remove the stalk and seeds, and put them on a grill tray. Grill them, skin side up, for about 10 minutes or until the skin is blistering and blackening. Remove from the tray, put into a bowl, cover with cling film and leave for about 10 minutes. Remove the skin with your fingers or by scraping with a knife.

2 Cut the peppers into rough 1cm dice and put them in a bowl with the tomatoes, spring onions, olive oil, vinegar, garlic and preserved lemon. Season with salt and freshly ground black pepper, and mix well. Taste the salad and add a little of the juice from the preserved lemon to taste.

3 Preheat the grill to its hottest temperature. Brush the sardines with olive oil and rub about ½ teaspoon of ras el hanout into the skin of each. Season the fish with some sea salt and freshly ground black pepper. Grill the fish for about 3 minutes on each side until the skin begins to crisp.

4 Serve with the salad and some good crusty bread.

SERVES 4

2 large green peppers
3 ripe tomatoes, skinned, deseeded and cut into rough 1cm dice
4 spring onions, chopped
6 tbsp extra-virgin olive oil, plus more for brushing
2 tbsp white wine vinegar
1 small garlic clove, crushed
peel from 1 large or 2 small preserved lemons, cut into small dice
salt and freshly ground black pepper
8 sardines, cleaned
2 tsp ras el hanout

OTHER SUITABLE FISH: anchovies, herrings, mackerel, pilchards

Fish tagine

SERVES 4

1kg monkfish or huss on the
   bone, skinned and cut into 3cm
   slices
salt and freshly ground white
   pepper
flour, for dusting
vegetable oil, for frying
1 tbsp olive oil
2 large onions, roughly chopped
4 garlic cloves, crushed
1 red chilli, deseeded and finely
   chopped
1 tbsp finely chopped root ginger
1 tsp ground cumin
1/2 tsp paprika
1/2 tsp crushed fennel seeds
good pinch of saffron strands
4 tomatoes, skinned, deseeded
   and roughly diced
1 tsp tomato purée
1 litre fish stock (page 52 or a
   good-quality fish stock cube
   dissolved in that amount of hot
   water)
1 large fennel bulb, cored and
   quartered
1 preserved lemon, halved
1 tbsp chopped coriander

Moroccan food is still relatively unknown here and for that reason often misinterpreted. The food is not so spicy and generally quite light, unless you fill yourself with couscous, that is. 'Spicy' shouldn't always mean 'hot', and subtle spices like fennel and saffron give a delicate fragrance to tagines, especially of fish. If you have a conical tagine dish, this can be cooked – or at least finished – and served in it.

1 Season the fish pieces and lightly flour them. Heat some vegetable oil in a non-stick or heavy frying pan and sauté them for 2–3 minutes on each side until lightly coloured. Remove from the pan and set aside.

2 Meanwhile, heat the olive oil in a heavy-based frying pan. Stir in the onions, garlic, chilli, ginger and spices. Cover and cook gently for 7–8 minutes until soft. Add the tomatoes, tomato purée and stock, season with salt and pepper, and simmer for 30 minutes. Then add the fennel and simmer gently for 30–35 minutes more, until the fennel is tender.

3 Add the fish, preserved lemon and coriander to the sauce and simmer for a further 10 minutes. Adjust the seasoning if necessary.

OTHER SUITABLE FISH: any firm-fleshed fish on or off the bone, any shellfish

Monkfish fillets with summer vegetables

Monkfish is now regarded as a luxury fish – and so it should be. The flesh is firm and lends itself to lots of different cooking methods. You can buy monkfish cheeks – as you might expect, little nuggets of meat from the cheeks of the fish – which would also be perfect for this dish. Pea shoots, also called mangetout leaves, are the really tasty tips of the pea plant, and you can buy them wherever there are good supplies of Oriental vegetables – and sometimes even at better supermarkets.

SERVES 4

200g (podded weight) broad beans

salt and freshly ground white pepper

100g (podded weight) peas

1 tsp caster sugar

16 thin asparagus tips

4 monkfish fillets, each about 200g

2 tbsp dry white wine

4 tbsp olive oil

handful of pea shoots (optional)

1 tbsp chopped chervil

1 tbsp chopped chives

1 Cook the broad beans in boiling salted water for 2 minutes, drain and refresh in cold water, then remove the outer skins if the beans are large.

2 Cook the peas in a little boiling salted water with the sugar for 4-5 minutes until tender, then drain and refresh in cold water. Drain well and mix with the beans.

3 Cook the asparagus tips in boiling salted water for 2-3 minutes until tender, refresh in cold water, drain well and mix with the rest of the vegetables.

4 Preheat the oven to 200ºC/gas 6. Cut each of the monkfish fillets into 3 evenly sized pieces and put them in an ovenproof dish with the white wine and olive oil. Season with salt and pepper, cover with a tight-fitting lid or foil and cook for 25 minutes, or until the fillets are just cooked.

5 Stir in the mixed vegetables, pea shoots and herbs, and return to the oven for 5 minutes.

6 Serve the fish in deep plates with the vegetables and cooking liquor spooned over.

OTHER SUITABLE FISH: any firm-fleshed fish

Steamed fillets of John Dory with baby leeks

illustrated on previous page

SERVES 4

4 fillets of John Dory, with the
   skin on, each about 160–180g
sea salt and freshly ground white
   pepper
250g baby leeks
2–3 tbsp extra-virgin olive oil
1/2 tbsp chopped chives
1/2 tbsp chopped parsley
juice of 1/3 lemon

The beautiful looks of the John Dory are reflected in its eating. It even has a distinguishable beauty spot on the flesh, which is apparently the reason for its being named *Saint-Pierre* in France and *pez de San Pedro* in Spain – the most common explanation for this is that the distinctive marks were left by St Peter's fingers when he threw the fish back into the water after hearing it making noises of distress.

1 Each fillet of John Dory conveniently divides itself into 3 smaller fillets lengthways along the fillet. With a sharp knife, separate the fillets, cutting through the skin.

2 Season the fillets with sea salt and freshly ground white pepper, lay them on a plate that fits in the steamer to catch the juices and steam them with a lid on for 5–6 minutes until just cooked. If you don't have a steamer, simply use a large pan with a tight-fitting lid and set the plate of fish on a trivet, or something else that will hold it clear of the water.

3 Meanwhile, plunge the baby leeks into a large pan of boiling salted water and simmer for 5 minutes. Drain in a colander and season with salt and freshly ground white pepper.

4 Mix any cooking juices from the fish with the olive oil, herbs and lemon juice. Arrange the John Dory fillets on warmed plates, intertwining them with the baby leeks. Spoon the olive oil and herb liquid over the top.

Variation   This dish is also delicious if you replace the baby leeks with sea kale. Sea kale is a fairly rare sea vegetable, especially if you are trying to buy it. You can find it growing wild in among rocks, but it can be bitter unless you catch the stems young and cover them with sand so they become blanched (don't tell your mates though). This does happen naturally by dint of the wind blowing sand around the stems, and the plants can blanch themselves by growing up between rocks, but you will need a keen eye open to spot the tops. Before you cook the kale, halve any long stems.

OTHER SUITABLE FISH: *brill, monkfish, porgy, turbot, any firm white fish*

Fillet of pollack with samphire & cockles

For reasons of conservation, we are being encouraged not to cook cod and other popular fish that we have been used to eating regularly, and that's why you are seeing some odd varieties of fish cropping up on menus and in recipes. It was bound to happen sooner or later. There are only so many fish in the sea and so many nations are still legally allowed to land fish of minuscule size, it doesn't help at all. I won't go on, because you have probably read enough about the situation, but the one upside of it all is that we are quickly learning that there are some previously overlooked – but equally tasty – species out there just waiting their turn.

For instance, pollack is an excellent alternative to cod. Try to buy fillets from a large fish, as it will be less flaky and easier to cook. Cockles are not used that much fresh, probably because of those seaside memories of sand and vinegar in polystyrene containers. If you can find live cockles (clams or mussels will do if you can't), they will need washing well to remove any sand. The best way to do this is to keep them under cold running water for an hour, giving them an occasional stir with your hand to allow them to release as much sand as possible and help you to enjoy the experience.

1 Lightly season the fish with salt and pepper. Heat a little oil in a large non-stick pan and fry the pieces for about 3 minutes on each side, until they are nicely coloured (if the fillets are very thick, you will need to finish them in a hot oven for another 5–10 minutes).

2 Meanwhile, give the cockles or clams a final rinse and put them into a large pan with the white wine and fish stock. Cover with a tight-fitting lid and cook over a high heat until they begin to open, shaking the pan and giving them an occasional stir. Drain the cockles in a colander, reserving the liquid and pouring it back into the pan.

3 Boil to reduce the liquid by half, then add the samphire. Return the cockles to the pan (they will not need seasoning as the samphire will do that) and stir well.

4 To serve, carefully remove the pollack from the pan with a fish slice and spoon the clams, samphire and liquid over the top.

SERVES 4

4 fillets from a large pollack,
  each about 200g, skinned and
  any residual bones removed
salt and freshly ground white
  pepper
olive oil, for cooking
200g cockles or clams, well
  rinsed
100ml white wine
100ml fish stock (page 52, or a
  corner of a fish stock cube
  dissolved in that amount of hot
  water)
200g samphire

OTHER SUITABLE FISH: any firm white fish

Salt-baked sea bass

This traditional way of cooking firm-textured fish like bass, bream and snapper produces delicious results. It seals the entire fish in completely, so it cooks without any juices or flavour escaping. Although it's a very simple method, it's unusual to find it on a restaurant menu here; normally you only see the process being used in Spain or Sicily.

When we opened J. Sheekey we thought we really had to have a dish like this on the menu but, because of space restrictions, it had to be quick to serve without losing the theatre of the cracking of the salt crust. After some months we ended up with a version using boned fish, which meant that once the salt was removed the fish could be cut in half and served quickly.

At home you could get away with an unfilleted fish if you're confident about serving it at the table. Otherwise, ask the fishmonger to bone the bass from the belly, leaving the head and tail on – a bit like a kipper – and removing the backbone and the small pin bones that run down the fillets. Depending on the size of your oven you may need to buy two smaller fish.

1 An hour before you want to cook, add a cup of water to the salt and mix well. Spread a thin layer of salt on a baking tray or oven-to-table dish. Fill the fish's stomach with the some of the herbs and season with pepper. Lay the bass on the salt and pack the rest of it in a 1cm layer all over the fish, firming it in place. Leave for an hour to drain.

2 Preheat the oven to 250°C/gas 9. Drain off any excess water from around the fish. Bake for 45 minutes, then remove from the oven.

3 If feeling confident, you can serve it in front of your guests. Otherwise, hide in the kitchen to cut it – perhaps after showing them it as it comes out of the oven. Have warmed plates ready and a large plate for the bits. Crack the salt a couple of times with the back of a heavy knife, then carefully scrape it away from the fish, removing as much as possible. Remove the head and tail, and cut the fish through the body into even portions, giving the underside a final check for salt before transferring them to warm plates.

4 Serve drizzled with some olive oil or melted butter and with some more fresh chopped dill or fennel.

SERVES 4-6

1kg coarse sea salt or
   Sel de Guérande
1 whole sea bass, about 2.5kg,
   scaled and boned as described
   opposite
fennel tops or a few sprigs
   of dill
freshly ground white
   pepper
olive oil or melted butter,
   to serve

OTHER SUITABLE FISH: bream (daurade), grouper, snapper

Thai baked fish

The sudden boom in Thai cooking has led to a lot of Asian shops – and even supermarket chains – stocking banana leaves. If you can't find them, then foil or greaseproof paper will do the job. Asian herbs are also becoming easier to find in supermarkets; some even sell prepared packets of Thai herb and spice mix.

Fish like sea bass, grouper and snapper are good fish to pitch against Thai flavours, but you can really use most luxury fish – or even humble fish like grey mullet – for this dish.

1 Preheat the oven to 200°C/gas 6. First, make the dipping sauce: heat the sesame oil in a pan and fry the chilli, galangal, lemon grass, lime leaves and garlic gently for 1 minute to soften them and release their flavours. Add the soy sauce, bring to the boil, then allow to cool and pour into a bowl or, ideally, individual dipping sauce dishes.

2 Now make the fragrant rice: cook the lemon grass with the lime leaves in about 1 litre of simmering salted water for 10 minutes. Add the rice and simmer for 10-12 minutes more until it is just cooked. Drain in a colander, then return the rice to the pan, cover it with a lid and then let it stand for 10 minutes before serving. This will help it become nice and fluffy.

3 While the rice is cooking, prepare the fish: heat the sesame oil in a pan and gently cook the chopped chilli, lemon grass, galangal, garlic, lime leaves and ground cumin in it for a couple of minutes until the aromatics are soft. Then tip the pan's contents into a food processor with the coriander and Thai basil, together with a couple of tablespoons of water, and blend to a paste. Spread the paste on the fish fillets and wrap each one in a piece of banana leaf like a parcel, folding the leaf so that the edges join underneath the fillet. Bake for 10-15 minutes, until the tip of a skewer inserted into the centre of a parcel comes out hot.

4 Place a fish parcel on each plate with a little pot of the dipping sauce. Serve the rice either in individual bowls or in a large bowl to be passed around.

SERVES 4

1 tbsp light (not toasted) sesame oil

1 small mild chilli, deseeded and roughly chopped

1 lemon grass stalk, peeled and the bulbous end roughly chopped

20g galangal or root ginger, peeled and roughly chopped

2 garlic cloves, crushed

4 lime leaves, roughly chopped

1/2 tsp ground cumin

10g coriander leaves

20g Thai basil

4 fish fillets (see above), each about 200g, with skin, scaled and any residual bones removed

1 banana leaf, about 1 metre in size

for the dipping sauce

1 tbsp sesame oil

1 small red chilli, deseeded and finely chopped

1 tbsp finely chopped galangal or root ginger

1 tbsp finely chopped lemon grass

2 lime leaves

1 garlic clove, crushed

3 tbsp soy sauce

for the fragrant rice

2 lemon grass stalks, bulbous ends crushed

8 lime leaves

salt

225g basmati rice, rinsed well in cold water

OTHER SUITABLE FISH: grey mullet, grouper, sea bass, sea bream, snapper, most fish

Roasting & baking fish   Some fish really benefit from being cooked whole in the oven, as this way they retain more of their moisture, true flavour and nutrients. This type of cooking method should be used with firmer-fleshed fish, such as sea bass, snapper, grouper and daurade, which also have fewer bones to contend with – bones being the negative aspect of fish cooked whole.

Serving a whole fish for 6–8 people can look very impressive, particularly if it is *stuffed (1)* with herb sprigs and garlic cloves or dried fennel sticks, and drizzled with some extra-virgin olive oil. To prevent the fish from drying out, it is also an idea to baste it occasionally with the pan juices, and this also helps build flavour.

Try *scoring cuts (2)* through the skin into the flesh (which also allows the heat to penetrate faster) and inserting lime or lemon slices into the cuts, or *rubbing spices (3)* into the skin before roasting. You can visit various countries by using various spice mixes, like *ras el hanout* and *chermoula* from North Africa or Thai spices.

Ask your fishmonger to scale the fish, cut the fins off and remove the stomach. The head can be left on or removed, depending on how squeamish you are. When cooking whole fish on the bone, allow about 40 minutes per kilo and use a hot oven (230°C/gas 8).

Another way of cooking fish that preserves even more of the flavour and nutrients and looks spectacular at the table is to bake them *en papillote*: that is, wrapped loosely in a tightly sealed parcel of greaseproof paper or foil. Some aromatic ingredients, like onions or shallots, garlic and herbs, are usually included in the parcel and a splash of stock or wine added just before the parcel is sealed. The contents then really steam more than bake, and the parcels are presented at the table so each person can open their own and revel in the wonderful aroma that rises from inside. A similar principle is involved when fish are baked wrapped in banana or other leaves, as in the Thai Baked Fish on page 117.

Serve the fish as simply as possible, perhaps with a salad, simply cooked potatoes and a butter- or oil-based sauce. You can also make a *quick pan sauce*, as you make gravies for meat roasts, by adding a little white wine, stock, butter or olive oil to the roasting pan and stirring and scraping up the sediment with a wooden spoon. If you like, you can even thicken this with a little cornflour mixed to a paste with water (simmer gently for a minute to cook out the flour taste) or some double cream.

1

2

3

Salt & pepper tiger prawns

SERVES 4 AS A STARTER

450g large headless raw tiger
    prawns in the shell

4 tbsp light (untoasted) sesame
    oil

1½ tsp sea salt

1½ tsp Szechuan peppercorns,
    crushed

1 bunch of spring onions, trimmed
    and cut into three

3 garlic cloves, crushed

1 small red chilli, deseeded and
    finely chopped

These aromatic prawns also make great nibbles to serve with drinks if you buy the smaller ones. If you like, you can leave the shells on the prawns and just cut through the shell to devein them (see page 12), which is the way I prefer it – as with most shellfish, getting your hands messy is part of the pleasure.

1 With a sharp serrated knife, cut down the back of the prawns through the shell and about 5mm into the flesh, and give them a rinse under cold running water to remove the black intestinal vein, then pat dry on some kitchen paper.

2 Heat 3 tablespoons of the sesame oil in a wok or heavy-based frying pan and fry the prawns on a high heat for 1–2 minutes. Add the salt and Szechuan peppercorns, and continue cooking for a couple minutes, stirring every so often. Remove the prawns from the pan and keep them warm.

3 Heat the rest of the sesame oil in the same pan and fry the spring onions, garlic and chilli for 1 minute. Stir in the prawns and serve.

OTHER SUITABLE FISH: shrimp

Sashimi of scallops with seaweed salad

Raw scallops have a wonderful naturally sweet taste. They must be live, though, and in the shells when you buy them. Get your fishmonger to open and clean them for you. The best seaweed comes dried from Oriental supermarkets. They even do mixes that are perfect here as the packets contain seaweeds of different colours.

1 Reconstitute the seaweed as per the instructions on the packet, then drain in a colander and pat dry with some kitchen paper.

2 Mix the soy sauce, vinegar and mirin together, and mix with the seaweed and samphire if in season, reserving a little for the scallops.

3 Arrange the seaweed in the scallop shells and put on serving dishes. Slice each scallop into 3 or 4 pieces and arrange on the seaweed, then spoon the reserved soy sauce mixture over the top.

SERVES 4

about 20g dried mixed seaweeds

1/2 tbsp good-quality light soy sauce

1 tbsp rice vinegar

1/2 tbsp mirin

60g samphire, trimmed (optional)

4 large scallops, cleaned and the cupped shell reserved

OTHER SUITABLE FISH: a wide range of fish and shellfish

Steamed scallops & tiger prawns with black bean sauce

SERVES 4 AS A STARTER

4 large or 8 medium headless
   raw tiger prawns, deveined and
   shelled, leaving the tail on
4 large scallops or 8 medium
   ones, cleaned in the cupped
   half-shell
sea salt and freshly ground white
   pepper
good handful of well-cleaned
   seaweed (if available)

for the dressing
2 tbsp Chinese fermented black
   beans, soaked in warm water
   for an hour, then drained
3 spring onions, thinly sliced
1/2 tbsp finely grated root ginger
2 garlic cloves, crushed
1 tbsp chopped coriander
1 tbsp rice wine
1 tbsp light soy sauce
1 tbsp groundnut or sunflower oil

There is something satisfying about serving scallops in their natural state instead of using the shells for ashtrays. Scallops can be a bit tricky to open, especially when really fresh – which, of course, they should be. So I recommend you ask your fishmonger to open them and give them a bit of a clean for you.

1 First make the dressing by mixing all of the ingredients together.

2 Put a tiger prawn into the shell with each scallop, season with salt and pepper, and steam for 4-5 minutes in a steamer, or you can use a roasting tray containing a couple of centimetres of boiling water and covered with a lid or foil set on the hob.

3 Serve the shells set on a little seaweed, if you can get it, to stop them wobbling around, then spoon over the dressing.

OTHER SUITABLE FISH: *clams, cockles, lobster, mussels, razor clams*

Moules marinière

SERVES 4

4-6 large shallots, finely chopped

5-6 garlic cloves, crushed

1 glass of white wine

150ml fish stock (page 52, or
1/4 of a good-quality fish stock
cube dissolved in that amount
of hot water)

salt and freshly ground black
pepper

2kg mussels, scrubbed and
debearded, discarding any that
stay stubbornly open when
tapped

2 tbsp chopped parsley

Generally you can get mussels most of the year round, although – as with oysters – when the water is warm, they get broody and will not be at their best for eating, and certain fisheries will not harvest them in order to give them a chance to breed. This recipe is the simplest and quickest way to enjoy mussels, but another nice option is to serve them mixed with cockles and/or clams.

You can add cream to a classic moules marinière to give a luxurious finish, or you can imbue your mussels with flavours from around the world, as, for example, in the steamed Catalan mussels variation below or by adding Thai spices and finishing the dish with coconut milk.

1 Put the shallots, garlic, white wine and fish stock into a large saucepan. Bring to the boil, season with salt and pepper, and add the mussels and parsley.

2 Cover with a lid and cook on a high heat, stirring occasionally, until all the mussels have opened (one or two may not, so don't keep cooking just for them once most have opened; simply discard the closed ones). Serve immediately.

Variation I first encountered Steamed Catalan Mussels on Spain's Costa Brava, near St Feluie de Guixolles. Most of the restaurants in the area served a version of it and each one was slightly different in its flavourings. The best one I had certainly had a distinct North African influence, containing ginger and cumin. I like the way that spices cross over in so many countries, especially when you are not expecting it.

Replace the shallots with a small onion, chopped, and cook that and the garlic in 4 tablespoons olive oil with 1/2 tablespoon finely chopped fresh ginger and 1 teaspoon each crushed fennel seeds and ground cumin until softened. Add a good pinch of saffron strands, 1 tablespoon tomato purée, 150g canned chopped tomatoes with their liquid, the white wine and 1 litre of stock. Simmer for 10-15 minutes and then season to taste. Add the mussels and parsley. Cover and cook as above.

OTHER SUITABLE FISH: clams, cockles, razor clams

Seafood salad

Seafood salad can be made with various fish and shellfish, depending on what's available. My preference is a mixture of prawns or lobster, squid, cuttlefish or octopus, scallops and perhaps some clams, mussels or razor clams to give it a bit of a lift. If you are struggling to get hold of such fish, then a couple of lightly cooked fillets of red mullet or gurnard give a good colour to the salad.

Samphire, just dipped in and out of boiling water, provides perfect crunch and colour; if it's not in season, some baby leeks would work well.

1 Put the mussels or clams in a pan with the fish stock and olive oil, and season with salt and pepper. Cover with a lid and cook on a high heat for 3–4 minutes, stirring occasionally, until they have all opened (one or two may not, so don't keep cooking just for them once most have opened, simply discard the closed ones). Remove from the heat and strain the cooking liquor through a fine-meshed sieve to remove any grit.

2 Rinse the pan and put the strained cooking liquor in it, together with the prawns and squid or cuttlefish. Cover and cook for 2 minutes. Add the scallops, stir well and cook, covered, for 1 minute, then remove from the heat and leave to cool.

3 Meanwhile, blanch the samphire in boiling unsalted water for 10 seconds and refresh in cold water; if you are using leeks, cook them in boiling salted water for 4–5 minutes until tender, then drain.

4 Remove the cooked prawns, squid and scallops from the cooking liquor and mix them in a bowl with the dressing ingredients and the mussels or clams.

5 Simmer the cooking liquor until the stock has almost all evaporated and just the oil is left. Leave to cool for a few minutes, then stir into the seafood mixture with the samphire or leeks and season lightly with salt and pepper, if necessary. Leave to stand for about 30 minutes before serving.

SERVES 4

150g mussels or clams, rinsed in cold running water and debearded, discarding any open ones that stay stubbornly open when handled

4 tbsp fish stock (page 52, or a corner of a good-quality fish stock cube dissolved in that amount of hot water)

4 tbsp olive oil

salt and freshly ground white pepper

8 raw tiger prawns, shelled and deveined

200g cleaned squid or cuttlefish, cut into rough 4–5cm squares

4 large scallops, cleaned, with any coral left on and the scallop cut in half horizontally

100g samphire, woody stalks trimmed, or 8 baby leeks, halved

for the dressing

juice of 1/2 lemon

1/2 tbsp chopped dill

1/2 tbsp chopped chervil

OTHER SUITABLE FISH: crab claws, cuttlefish or octopus, gurnard, lobster, razor clams, red mullet

Roasted shellfish with aïoli

SERVES 4

2 small live lobsters, each
   weighing about 400g

4 large whole raw tiger prawns

4 razor clams and/or a couple of
   handfuls of carpet shell
   clams (palourdes) or British
   surf clams

about 150ml olive oil

sea salt and freshly ground black
   pepper

4 scallops, cleaned in the cupped
   half shell

handful of cockles

8 spring onions, halved

4 garlic cloves, crushed

2 tbsp chopped parsley

1 recipe quantity aïoli (page 50)

I can't think of a better main course than this to be tucking into while dining by the sea. A glass or two of a crisp dry white or rosé or Champagne and some good company is all you need – and finger bowls and crackers, of course. You can vary the elements of the dish depending on where you are and what's available. Langoustines or cigales (flat lobsters) can be added, and even crab claws. In season I throw in a handful of samphire at the end, or you can just use spring onions, garlic shoots or baby leeks. Grilled on a portable barbecue on the beach, this will raise a few eyebrows, especially with the Champagne bucket buried in the sand alongside!

1 First prepare your shellfish for roasting. If squeamish about cutting live things in half, then ask your fishmonger to chop the lobsters in half lengthwise and crack the claws for easy access to the meat once it's cooked. Alternatively, plunge them into boiling water for a minute to kill them, remove them from the pan and run them under cold water for 1 minute, then proceed as above. (Incidentally, both the rapid splitting in half and the boiling water techniques are recommended by the RSPCA as swift humane methods of dispatch.) The tiger prawns can be left whole or you can peel them if you wish. Prepare and cook the razor clams as in the recipe on page 148, but don't worry about the wine, herbs, etc., and only trim the sac and leave them whole.

2 Preheat the oven to 230°C/gas 8 and preheat a roasting tray large enough to take all the shellfish in a single layer (or two if necessary) with a couple of tablespoons of olive oil in it.

3 Season the lobsters and put them into the hot roasting tray, flesh side down. Cook for 6-7 minutes in the oven, then turn them over. Add the scallops, prawns, clams, cockles and spring onions, and season with salt and pepper. Mix the rest of the olive oil with the garlic and spoon over all of the shellfish. Put back in the oven for another 7-8 minutes, then remove from the oven and mix in the parsley. Add some more olive oil if you wish, as the shellfish tend to absorb it.

4 Arrange the shellfish on a warm serving platter or individual serving plates and spoon the cooking juices and oil over. Serve with the Aïoli.

OTHER SUITABLE FISH: any mollusc

6 posh*fish*

Eggs royale

This is an extremely indulgent twist on eggs benedict that is perfect for a celebratory breakfast or brunch with a glass or two of bubbly. Hollandaise can be a bit tricky if you haven't made it before, so you may want to practise on your own before serving it to your guests. For a less expensive version you could use salmon eggs instead of the caviar, and you could even use cold-smoked trout instead of the smoked salmon.

1 First make the hollandaise sauce: put the vinegar, shallot, herbs and peppercorns in a saucepan with 2 tablespoons of water and reduce the liquid to about a dessertspoonful. Strain it and set aside.

2 Gently melt the butter in a heavy-based pan and simmer it gently for 5-10 minutes until it looks like it is separating. Remove it from heat and leave it to cool a little, then pour off the pure butter on top that has separated from the whey at the bottom and discard the whey. Using butter clarified in this way helps to keep the sauce thick.

3 Put the egg yolks into a small non-reactive bowl with half of the vinegar reduction and whisk over a pan of gently simmering water until the mixture begins to thicken and become frothy. Slowly trickle in the butter, whisking continuously (an electric hand-held whisk will help). Take care as, if the butter is added too quickly, the sauce will separate.

4 When you have added two-thirds of the butter, taste the sauce and add a little more - or all - of the reduction and season with salt and pepper. Then add the rest of the butter as before. The sauce should not be too vinegary, but the vinegar should just cut the oiliness of the butter. Adjust the seasoning, if necessary, then lay some cling film directly on the surface of sauce to stop it forming a skin and leave in a warm (not hot) place until needed. The sauce can be reheated briefly over a bowl of hot water and lightly whisked again, but try to avoid this.

5 To serve, lightly toast the muffins and soft-poach the eggs. Place a slice of smoked salmon on each muffin half with a poached egg on top and coat it with a couple of generous spoonfuls of the sauce and as much caviar as you want.

SERVES 4

2 English muffins, halved

4 large eggs

4 slices of smoked salmon, about 100-125g in total

30g or more Sevruga, Beluga or Osietre caviar

for the hollandaise sauce

1 tbsp white wine vinegar

1 small shallot, roughly chopped

a few sprigs tarragon

1 bay leaf

5 black peppercorns

250g unsalted butter

2 large egg yolks

salt and freshly ground white pepper

OTHER SUITABLE FISH: cold smoked trout, salmon eggs

Omelette Arnold Bennett

SERVES 4

200g undyed smoked haddock
    fillet

1 large shallot, finely chopped

1 tbsp chopped dill

1 tsp Dijon mustard

200ml double cream

salt and freshly ground white
    pepper

8 large eggs, beaten, plus 1 extra
    egg yolk

good knob of butter

This is one of those old classics that was created by the customer and not the chef. It was, in fact, requested at the Savoy Hotel for the writer and critic whose name has been well stamped on the dish. It doesn't appear on too many restaurant menus, which is a shame because, made well, it's a real delight. Omelettes can be a pain in busy restaurants, as the minute you get one on order the kitchen goes into disarray. Try to buy good-quality undyed smoked haddock, as God alone knows what's in the bright yellow stuff.

1 Put the fish and shallot in a pan and just cover with water. Bring to the boil, cover and simmer for 2 minutes. Remove fish with a slotted spoon and drain on kitchen paper. Carefully remove the skin and any bones.

2 Continue to simmer the cooking liquid until almost completely reduced, then add 150ml of the cream and the mustard. Bring back to the boil and continue to simmer until it has reduced by two-thirds and has thickened. Remove from the heat and leave to cool a little.

3 Flake the haddock into the sauce, stir in the dill and season with salt and white pepper. Preheat the grill to maximum.

4 In a bowl set over a pan of simmering water, whisk the egg yolk and remaining cream until light and frothy but not starting to cook, then remove the bowl from the pan and set aside.

5 Heat a little butter in a small non-stick frying or blini pan over a low heat. Season the beaten eggs and pour a quarter of the egg mix into the pan, or enough to two-thirds fill it. Over a low heat, stir the eggs with a wooden spoon or plastic spatula, until the mix begins to set but the eggs are still soft. Stop stirring to let the bottom set slightly.

6 Turn a plate a little larger than the pan upside down on top of it. Invert the omelette on to the plate and transfer to a heatproof plate or serving dish. Repeat with the remaining mixture to make 3 more.

7 Mix the whisked egg and cream into the haddock mixture and spoon over the omelettes, spreading it evenly with the back of the spoon until covered. Put under the grill for a minute or two until evenly browned.

OTHER SUITABLE FISH: any hot-smoked fish

Fillet of sea bass with lobster mash

I can't quite remember how lobster mash came about, but we certainly use it a lot in the restaurants - we even make a mash with crayfish and shrimps too. This is a good way to use lobsters that have died on you, or lobster meat left from a feast when people have been too lazy to tackle the claws.

1 Cook the lobster as described on page 12 and remove all the meat, reserving the shells. Chop the meat into smallish pieces and set aside.

2 To make the sauce: in a large heavy-based saucepan, fry the lobster shells, shallots and garlic in the oil over a medium heat for about 6-7 minutes, until they begin to colour lightly. Add the butter and flour and stir well into the shells. Add the saffron, tarragon and tomato purée, and stir well. Gradually stir in the white wine and hot fish stock and bring to the boil. Simmer for about 10 minutes until the sauce has reduced by about half, then add the cream. Season lightly with salt and pepper, bring to the boil and simmer gently for about 30 minutes, until the sauce has reduced by half and has a good thick consistency.

3 Strain the sauce through a colander into a bowl and stir the shells with a spoon to ensure all the sauce goes through. Remove about 10 per cent of the shells (about half a cupful) and blend with the strained sauce in a liquidizer. Strain through a fine-meshed sieve.

4 At the same time as making the sauce, cook the potatoes in boiling salted water until just tender, drain and dry off in the hot pan. Crush them with a fork and mix with the lobster meat, tarragon and 4-5 tablespoons of the lobster sauce. Add the butter, season with salt and pepper and heat up slowly, stirring every so often.

5 Meanwhile, season the sea bass and lightly flour the skin side. Heat the vegetable oil in a non-stick pan and cook the fillets, skin side down, for 4 minutes until crisp, then turn them over and cook the other side for 2-3 minutes, until the fish is just cooked through.

6 Spoon the mash on to the centre of 4 warmed plates and place the fish on top the mash, skin side up. Reheat the sauce and pour around.

SERVES 4

1 small lobster, about 300-400g or smaller
250g small waxy potatoes, such as Charlotte or Roseval, peeled
1 tbsp chopped tarragon
good knob of butter
4 sea bass fillets from a large fish, each about 160-180g, skin left on and scaled, and any residual bones removed
flour, for dusting
vegetable oil, for frying

for the lobster sauce
4 shallots, roughly chopped
1 garlic clove, chopped
vegetable oil, for frying
good knob of butter
2 tsp flour
good pinch of saffron strands
a few sprigs of tarragon
1-2 tbsp tomato purée
4 tbsp white wine
200ml fish stock (page 52, or $\frac{1}{4}$ good-quality fish stock cube dissolved in that amount of hot water)
350ml double cream
salt and freshly ground black pepper

OTHER SUITABLE FISH: any firm-fleshed white fish, such as cod, halibut, snapper or turbot

Pork-stuffed sea bream with ginger sauce

In Oriental cooking, the mixing of pork and fish is quite common. Here it gives quite an unusual twist to a neutral-tasting fish. Fatty pork like belly takes on Asian flavours well and, used in the empty cavity of a fish like sea bream or sea bass, makes a perfect dinner party sharing dish for serving together with some other Oriental-style dishes.

1 Preheat the oven to 220º/gas 7. Make the stuffing by mixing all of the ingredients together.

2 Fill the cavities of the fish with the stuffing, season both sides of the fish with salt and pepper and brush with vegetable oil.

3 Cook in the oven for about 30 minutes, or until the point of a skewer or small knife comes out hot when inserted into the centre of the fish.

4 While the fish is cooking, make the sauce: gently cook the root ginger, garlic and chilli in the oil for 2-3 minutes until soft. Add the fish sauce, soy sauce and 150ml water, and bring to the boil. Simmer gently for 5 minutes. Dilute the cornflour in a little water and stir into the sauce. Simmer for 2 minutes and then remove from the heat. The sauce should be a thick coating consistency; if not, simmer a little longer until it thickens.

5 To serve, pour the sauce over the fish or to one side of it.

Variations
If you don't fancy meat in the stuffing, you could replace the pork with chopped raw prawns or even a mix of chopped vegetables like shiitake mushrooms and spring onions.

Instead of the ginger sauce, you could use the black bean sauce on page 122.

SERVES 4

4 sea bream, each weighing about 350-400g, or 1 or 2 large ones, cleaned and scaled
vegetable oil, for brushing

for the stuffing
200g minced pork belly
4 spring onions, finely chopped
3 garlic cloves, crushed
1 lemon grass stalk, finely chopped
2 tbsp chopped coriander leaves
1 tbsp chopped root ginger or galangal
1 red chilli, deseeded and finely chopped
salt and freshly ground black pepper

for the ginger sauce
2 tbsp finely chopped root ginger
2 garlic cloves, crushed
1 red chilli, deseeded and finely chopped
1 tbsp light (untoasted) sesame oil or groundnut oil
2 tbsp fish sauce
1 tbsp light soy sauce
1 tsp cornflour

OTHER SUITABLE FISH: *catfish, sea bass, snapper*

Fillet of plaice belle meunière

illustrated on previous page

SERVES 4

250g soft herring roes, fresh or
    defrosted frozen

about 600ml milk

4 fillets of plaice from a large
    fish, each about 180-200g,
    skinned

salt and freshly ground white
    pepper

flour, for dusting

vegetable oil, for frying

200g butter

125g peeled cooked brown
    shrimps or prawns

1 tbsp chopped parsley

juice of 1/2 lemon

This is a classic dish from the days of *haute cuisine* that deserves revival. Sadly, many of the old recipes that appeared in Escoffier's *repertoire de cuisine* rarely surface now. I particularly like this combination, as the sweet brown shrimps complement the slightly bitter taste of the herring roes.

Try to find large plaice if possible, as they are less flaky than the smaller fish. They are, however, not so easy to come by, as they are often caught by divers with a spear gun, and can be the size of brill and turbot.

1 Put the soft roes into a saucepan, cover with the milk, bring to the boil and simmer for 2 minutes. Remove from the pan, discard the milk and put the roes on some kitchen paper to drain.

2 Season the plaice fillets on both sides with salt and pepper and fold them in half if they are from a small fish, to help prevent them overcooking. Lightly flour them and fry them in the vegetable oil in a non-stick or heavy-based frying pan for 3-4 minutes on each side, adding 50g of the butter when you turn them.

3 Meanwhile, heat a little more vegetable oil in another frying pan, season the soft roes with salt and pepper and fry them for 3-4 minutes over medium heat, turning them every so often until they begin to colour. Add the rest of the butter to the pan and, when it starts foaming (don't let it go brown), add the shrimps, parsley and lemon juice, and remove from the heat.

4 Using a fish slice or spatula, remove the plaice fillets from the pan and spoon the roes, shrimps and butter over the top.

OTHER SUITABLE FISH: *any white fish*

Hot-smoked salmon with horseradish potatoes

Braden rost ('roasted salmon' in Gaelic) is cured with sea salt and unrefined brown sugar, then smoked at an ambient temperature like traditional smoked salmon for 12 hours before extra fire boxes are lit and the fillets then cook through. *Braden rost* can be served hot, cold or warm, and the obvious accompaniment seems to be horseradish. It could be flaked into a salad with a horseradish-spiked dressing.

SERVES 4

400g small waxy potatoes, such as Roseval or Charlotte

2 tbsp hot good-quality horseradish sauce

4 tbsp mayonnaise (page 62 or good-quality bought)

4 spring onions, thinly sliced

salt and freshly ground black pepper

400-500g hot-smoked salmon (*braden rost*, see above left)

1 lemon, quartered

1 Cook the potatoes in their skins in boiling salted water until just tender, drain and allow to cool slightly, but peel while still warm.

2 With a fork, crush the potatoes in a bowl, again while still warm, then mix them with the horseradish, mayonnaise and spring onions, and season with salt and pepper.

3 Cut the salmon into 4 evenly sized pieces and arrange each on a serving plate alongside a pile of the potatoes and one of the lemon quarters.

OTHER SUITABLE FISH: smoked cod or haddock, home-smoked sea trout

Poached turbot with egg sauce

SERVES 4

4 turbot steaks (preferably middle cut) on the bone, each about 250-350g

for the court bouillon

1 leek, roughly chopped

1 onion, roughly chopped

2 celery stalks, roughly chopped

1 bay leaf

a few sprigs of thyme

1 tsp fennel seeds

1 tsp black peppercorns

2 tbsp dry white wine

salt and freshly ground black pepper

for the egg sauce

2 shallots, finely chopped

4 tbsp white wine

100ml fish stock (page 52, or ¼ good-quality fish stock cube dissolved in that amount of hot water)

400ml double cream

2 hard-boiled eggs, shelled and chopped

1 tbsp chopped chives

1 tbsp chopped parsley

In my days at the Dorchester this was a regular menu item in the Grill Room. We used to serve it in a nice silver pot and it would get lifted out in front of the customer and the egg sauce poured over. It is important that the sauce is quite thick or it will be diluted when the moisture comes out of the fish as it is removed from the bone. A hollandaise sauce (page 129) will work equally well.

Court bouillons – flavoured broths in which to poach fish and shellfish – vary considerably, depending on what you are cooking and how you are going to serve it. The flavourings can vary from peppercorns and fennel seeds to slightly stronger ones if you are poaching things like crayfish that have a tendency to be rather bland. Wine or a dash of wine vinegar can also be added for cold lobster or salmon dishes. The latter is better for shellfish as the flavour doesn't really penetrate through the shell and wine is preferable for fish as the flesh doesn't take on the flavour. If you don't add vinegar and instead include some chopped vegetables, like carrots and fennel, then you will have more of a vegetable court bouillon that may be used as the basis of a sauce.

1 First make the court bouillon: put the vegetables, herbs and spices in a pan and add 2.5 litres of water. Bring to the boil and simmer for 20 minutes. Add the wine and seasoning, and simmer for 10 minutes more. This can then be cooled and kept for up to a week in the refrigerator.

2 To make the sauce: put the shallots in a saucepan with the white wine and boil until the wine has almost completely evaporated. Add the fish stock and boil again until you have only about 3-4 tablespoons left. Add the cream, bring to the boil and simmer until it has reduced by about half and is quite thick. Add the egg and herbs, season with salt and pepper, and simmer for another minute.

3 While the sauce is being prepared, simmer the turbot in the court bouillon for about 10-12 minutes, until cooked through (the point of a sharp knife inserted into the thickest part of the fish will be hot to the tongue). Remove with a fish slice and drain on kitchen paper.

4 Serve the fish and the sauce separately or on the side.

OTHER SUITABLE FISH: *brill, monkfish, large plaice*

Rock eel bordelaise

What's posh about dogfish you may ask; quite rightly so, but a few years ago you might well have said the same of cod and monkfish. Both dogfish and smooth hound or tope are generally sold as huss or rock eel, and known to fishermen as dogfish. To add to the confusion, they are sold as rock salmon in fish and chip shops. Otherwise they are completely forgotten about. The fairly firm flesh will withstand a bit of braising and marinating. I've used a mixture of equal parts meat stock and fish stock here, but non-meat-eaters can just use all fish stock. Rock eel would normally be skinned before it gets ashore by the fisherman; ask the fishmonger to cut it into roughly 80g chunks on the bone.

1 First make the sauce: melt the butter in a heavy-based saucepan and gently cook the shallots, garlic and thyme in it until soft without allowing them to colour. Add the flour and stir well with a wooden spoon, then stir in the tomato purée. Slowly add the red wine, then gradually add both the stocks. Bring to the boil and simmer on a low heat for about 30 minutes.

2 Meanwhile, heat the oil in a heavy-based frying pan. Dust the pieces of fish with flour, season with salt and pepper and fry them, a few at a time, on all sides until well coloured. Remove from the pan and drain on some kitchen paper.

3 Clean the pan and sauté the mushrooms in the butter for a few minutes until lightly coloured, then drain in a colander.

4 Add the fish and mushrooms to the sauce and simmer for 10 minutes. The sauce should by now have thickened to a gravy-like consistency; if it hasn't, remove the pieces of fish and simmer the sauce until it has thickened, then return the fish to the sauce and adjust the seasoning with salt and pepper if necessary.

5 Serve with buttery mashed potato or rice.

SERVES 4

vegetable or corn oil, for frying

1kg rock eel, or whatever they call it (see left), cut as described

flour, for dusting

salt and freshly ground white pepper

150g wild mushrooms or button mushrooms, quartered or cut into rough chunks

good knob of butter

for the bordelaise sauce

30g butter

8 shallots, finely chopped

1 garlic clove, crushed

a few sprigs of thyme, leaves removed and chopped

2 tsp flour

1 tsp tomato purée

125ml red wine

250ml beef stock (or 1/2 good-quality beef stock cube dissolved in that amount of hot water)

250ml fish stock (page 52, or 1/2 good-quality fish stock cube dissolved in that amount of hot water)

OTHER SUITABLE FISH: eel or any firm-fleshed fish

Fillet of pike with sauce nantua

SERVES 4

4 skinned pike fillets, each about
    160-180g

salt and freshly ground white
    pepper

16-20 crayfish

olive oil, for frying or roasting

small knob of butter (optional)

sauce nantua (pages 102-3, using
    only half the flour), to serve

1/2 tbsp chopped tarragon

Quenelle de brochet nantua is a classic French dish in which both main ingredients – pike and crayfish – come from fresh water. Pike has an unusual bone structure, having not only a set of bones down its middle but two other sets, one on either side, and is a real pain to bone when raw. That's why most recipes with pike are made into a mousseline. If you can't get pike, then turbot, brill or its cousin the zander (pike perch) will do nicely.

I won't put you through the pain of making a mousse, but what I will do is share a top tip given to me by Mauro Bregoli, who for many years owned the brilliant Manor House in Romsey, Hampshire. It is best first to buy your pike filleted, unless you are a dab hand with a filleting knife. You'll have to order it from a fishmonger and it will then need to be skinned. Mauro suggests that you lightly steam the pike so the flesh shrinks to reveal the protruding ends of the bones, which can then much more easily be removed.

1 Season the pike fillets and steam for about 10 minutes. If you haven't got a steamer, preheat the oven to 190°C/gas 5, lay the fillets in a roasting tray with about 2cm of hot water, cover with foil and cook in the oven for 15 minutes. This steaming causes the flesh to shrink a little, leaving the bones protruding so they can be pulled out with a pair of pliers or tweezers. There are lots, so be patient – it's worth it.

2 Cook the crayfish in simmering salted water for 5 minutes, then plunge them into cold water. Remove the meat from the shells and the claws if they are big enough. Break the shells up a little with a heavy knife and use to make the sauce nantua.

3 Cook the pike fillets again. Either fry them in olive oil for 2-3 minutes on each side, then add a small knob of butter and continue to fry them until lightly browned; or preheat the oven to gas 200°C/gas 6, heat a couple of tablespoons of olive oil in a roasting pan and roast them for 10-12 minutes or until lightly coloured.

4 Meanwhile, if necessary, simmer the sauce until it has coating consistency, stir in the tarragon and drop in the peeled crayfish for a minute to re-heat them. To serve, spoon the sauce over the fish fillets.

OTHER SUITABLE FISH: *brill, turbot, zander or any firm-fleshed white fish*

Lobster with sweetbreads & tarragon

SERVES 4

2 lobsters, each about 500g, cooked (see page 12)

500ml beef stock (or a good-quality beef stock cube dissolved in that amount of hot water)

3 shallots, roughly chopped

1 bay leaf

1 garlic clove

400g veal sweetbreads

lobster sauce (page 131, made using the lobster shells)

salt and freshly ground black pepper

flour, for dusting

good knob of butter

1/2 tbsp chopped tarragon

This is a more sophisticated version of that American restaurant favourite 'surf and turf', which pairs lobster with steak. The subtle flavour of the sweetbreads together with that of the tarragon complements the lobster perfectly. The sauce for this dish is a basic shellfish sauce which is made like the sauce nantua on pages 102–3, using meat stock in place of some of the fish stock.

1 Remove the claws from the lobsters, then crack the shells, reserving them, and put the meat to one side. Remove the tail by twisting it away from the head, then, with a heavy knife, cut the tail in half lengthways.

2 In a large pan, bring the beef stock to the boil with the shallots, bay leaf and garlic. Add the sweetbreads, bring back to the boil, lower the heat and simmer for 10 minutes. Remove the sweetbreads with a slotted spoon and leave to cool on a plate. Reserve the cooking liquid for the sauce.

3 Using the shells and head from the lobster, make a sauce nantua as described on pages 102–3, replacing some of the fish stock with the reserved sweetbread cooking liquor.

4 Trim any fat from the sweetbreads and cut them into 2cm-thick slices. Season them with salt and pepper, lightly dust with flour and fry in some butter over a medium heat for 2 minutes on each side until golden, then drain on some kitchen paper.

5 Bring the sauce to the boil, add the lobster, sweetbreads and tarragon and simmer for 3–4 minutes. Serve with boiled or wild rice, green vegetables or boiled potatoes.

OTHER SUITABLE FISH: crayfish, langoustines, prawns, rock lobster

Scallops thermidor

Scallops, with their firm texture and sweet flavour, lend themselves to many types and styles of cooking. Ask your fishmonger if he has some seaweed and use it on the plates under the scallop shells to prevent them wobbling around.

1 First make the sauce: put the wine and shallots in a pan, bring to the boil and simmer until almost all of the wine has evaporated. Add the fish stock and reduce again similarly. Stir in 300ml of the double cream with the mustard and reduce until the sauce is thick enough to coat the back of spoon. Add the grated cheeses and whisk until the sauce is smooth. Season and leave to cool.

2 Whip the remaining cream until it forms soft peaks and fold it into the cool sauce with the tarragon and egg yolk.

3 Heat the olive oil in a large pan, add the spinach and season with salt and pepper. Cook over a high heat for just a couple minutes, stirring occasionally, until the spinach has softened. Transfer to a colander and leave to drain, pushing any excess liquid out with the back of a spoon.

4 Preheat the grill to its highest setting and heat the knob of butter in a non-stick pan until bubbling. Season the scallops with salt and pepper, and fry for 30–40 seconds on each side without allowing them to colour too much, then drain on some kitchen paper.

5 Divide the spinach between the scallop shells and place a scallop on each. Spoon the sauce over each scallop, put them on the grill tray and place under the very hot grill for 3–4 minutes until they brown. Serve immediately.

SERVES 4 AS A FIRST COURSE

1 tbsp olive oil

200g spinach, stalks removed

good knob of butter

12 medium-sized scallops, cleaned and the shells reserved

for the thermidor sauce

100ml white wine

4 shallots, finely chopped

200ml fish stock (page 52, or ¼ good-quality fish stock cube dissolved in that amount of hot water)

350ml double cream

2 tsp English mustard

40g Cheddar cheese, grated

20g freshly grated Parmesan cheese

salt and freshly ground white pepper

1 tsp chopped tarragon

1 egg yolk

OTHER SUITABLE FISH: any shellfish

Tempura prawns & asparagus

I often get cravings for tempura and just have to order it to get the urge out of my system. I can then, though, get bored of it halfway through and end up leaving much on my plate. Like most things, however, if you use interesting ingredients it excites the palate, and this sauce from the London Nobu Restaurant helps the cause.

1 First make the sauce: in a non-reactive bowl, whisk the egg yolks with the salt and pepper, then gradually trickle in the rice vinegar and oil until the sauce thickens. Add the sweet chilli garlic sauce.

2 Blanch the asparagus in boiling salted water for 2 minutes, then refresh in cold water, drain and pat dry.

3 Preheat vegetable or corn oil for deep-frying to 160-180°C. Holding them by the tails, dip the prawns in the batter and fry them in batches of 5-6 at a time for 2-3 minutes until crisp but not browned, stirring them in the oil every so often. Remove with a slotted spoon, drain on some kitchen paper and keep warm. Dip, fry and drain the asparagus tips in the same way.

4 Serve the prawns and asparagus mixed with the sauce in little pots.

SERVES 4 AS A STARTER

16 medium asparagus tips, cut to about 8-10cm long

vegetable or corn oil for deep-frying

8 medium-large tiger prawns, shelled with the tails left on and deveined

1 recipe quantity tempura batter (page 83)

for the sauce

2 egg yolks

good pinch of salt

freshly ground white pepper

2 tsp rice vinegar

200ml vegetable oil

1 tbsp (or more to taste) sweet chilli garlic sauce or sweet chilli sauce with a crushed small garlic clove mixed in

OTHER SUITABLE FISH: any shellfish or firm-fleshed fish

Steamed razor clams with chorizo & broad beans

illustrated on previous page

SERVES 4

1kg live razor clams
1/2 glass of dry white wine
a few sprigs of thyme
3 garlic cloves, roughly chopped
1 tsp salt
1 tbsp chopped parsley,
    reserving the stalks
250g broad beans, shelled
4 tbsp olive oil
115g cooking chorizo, sliced
    to the thickness of a coin
60g butter
pepper

Razor clams are an odd kind of shellfish not often seen on the fishmonger's slab. I first tried them in Spain, cooked very simply, and I've since discovered that simply is the only way to prepare these phallic-looking molluscs. It's important to use the soft cooking type of chorizo for this, as opposed to the hard dry sausage that is sliced and eaten as it is.

1 Rinse the razor clams well in cold running water for 10 minutes, discarding any that don't close when handled. Put them in a pot with the wine, thyme, garlic, salt and parsley stalks. Cover with a lid and cook over a high heat for a few minutes, stirring occasionally, until all the shells open. Drain in a colander and leave to cool.

2 Preheat the oven to 150°C/gas 2. Carefully remove the clams from the shells, keeping the shell intact (discard any that haven't opened). Cut away the central dark-looking intestinal sac and discard. Cut each clam into 4 or 5 pieces, place back in the shell and arrange the shells on a baking tray. Keep warm in the low oven.

3 Meanwhile, cook the broad beans in boiling salted water for 2 minutes, then drain in a colander. If they are large, they should be podded again.

4 Heat the olive oil in a pan and cook the chorizo on a low heat for 1-2 minutes. Add the broad beans, butter and chopped parsley, and season lightly with salt and pepper.

5 Put the clams in their shells on warmed serving plates and spoon the chorizo mixture over.

OTHER SUITABLE FISH: *clams, cuttlefish, mussels, squid*

Oysters

Oysters are very much a part of English history. Even the Romans loved our Colchester oysters so much they made Colchester, or Camulodunum, as it was then called, the capital of Roman England. Native Colchester oyster shells have been found in Rome during archaeological excavations. Most English folk nowadays, though, live in fear of oysters. We rarely eat them or even know where to start. How many people can prise open the shell to reveal that pure taste of the sea, or '*le gout de la mer*', as the French say?

Our English native season starts in September and lasts through the following months with an 'r' in them. September, though, is still a bit hit and miss, and October is generally held to be the best time to start eating them. Oysters are still broody until the water gets colder, when they will have released all their larvae, causing them to be milky and rather unpleasant in the mouth, although some people enjoy the experience (not me!).

Opening oysters

This is a tricky business if you haven't tackled it before, and can be a daunting experience, so expect several cuts, as it takes a few dozen oysters to develop the technique.

There are several different types of knife on the market and even various gadgets which aim to ease the pain. Beginners should really buy an oyster knife with a guard *(1, left)* and, as you become more experienced, you can move on to the slimmer blade without the guard *(1, right)*.

The object of the operation is first to prise open the shell at the hinge with the point of your knife and then to work the knife into the shell and sever the muscle on the flat part of the shell to release the meat intact on the curved shell.

Before you start, grab a cloth or tea towel and fold it a couple of times. Lay the oyster in the cloth (this should prevent the cuts) on a flat surface with the flat part of the shell facing up and the pointed hinge facing towards you. Holding the oyster down with the cloth and, folding some of the cloth back over your hand – just in case the knife slips – force the point of the oyster knife into the hinge of the shell, carefully moving the knife from side to side until you can feel the shell loosening – it will take a bit of force *(2)*. Keep the knife in the shell, twisting it a little, and run it along the top of the flat shell until you feel the muscle, which attaches the oyster to the shell. Cut this and you are done. You just need to remove and discard the flat shell *(3)* and remove any little bits of shell that may be on the oyster flesh – don't pour away the natural juices *(4)*.

You can loosen the flesh from the curved shell for your guests and flip it over, or let them do it themselves – I prefer the latter. Serve them on beds of seaweed or crushed ice, with lemon wedges and/or Tabasco sauce (green or red) or shallot vinegar.

For enough **shallot vinegar** to accompany 24 oysters: finely chop 4 shallots and then mix them with 100ml good-quality red wine vinegar (I recommend a Cabernet Sauvignon vinegar), then leave to infuse for 1 hour.

Alternatively, try an **American seafood sauce** with your oysters: simply mix 3 tablespoons of tomato ketchup with 2 tablespoons freshly grated horseradish (you can use the stuff that comes in jars but don't be tempted by ready-made horseradish sauce) and add lemon juice to taste. This is also really great with raw clams and cold lobster.

Fried oysters in angel hair with wasabi mayonnaise

I first experienced this dish at the Nobu Restaurant in London and then, fortunately, again on a trip to the Dom Perignon Champagne producers with four other chefs, including Mark Edwards of Nobu. We were invited for the weekend on the condition that we each cooked one dish for a dinner on the Saturday night. Mark knocked up this memorable creation of fried oysters which are simply wrapped in shredded Greek filo (*kadayif*), deep-fried and served with wasabi mixed with mayonnaise. The most difficult thing will probably be getting hold of the pastry. If you can't, you can use rice vermicelli that has been soaked in hot water until malleable.

1 Have a slightly damp tea towel or cloth ready to keep the pastry covered while you are working. Dip each oyster in the flour and water paste, allowing any excess to drain off, then pull long clumps off the pastry and wrap a layer firmly around the oyster, then set it on a tray.

2 Mix the wasabi with the mayonnaise and set side. Drain the seaweed and mix with the mirin or sake, then divide it up between the oyster shells.

3 Meanwhile, heat about 8cm of oil in a deep-fryer or heavy-based saucepan to 160-180°C. Fry the oysters a few at a time for about a minute, until lightly coloured, then drain on some kitchen paper. Put an oyster in each shell with about 1/2 teaspoon of the mayonnaise on top and serve immediately.

Variation   If you prefer, you can dress the fried oysters with a chilli mayonnaise; simply replace the wasabi with a quantity of good-quality chilli sauce to taste.

SERVES 4
200–250g kadayif (shredded filo pastry, see above left)
12 plump rock oysters, shucked and the shells reserved
2 tbsp flour mixed to a wet paste with cold water
1/2 tbsp freshly grated wasabi or 3/4 tbsp ready-made
2 tbsp good-quality bought mayonnaise
20g dried mixed seaweed (see page 121), reconstituted in cold water
1 tbsp mirin or sake
vegetable or corn oil, for deep-frying

OTHER SUITABLE FISH: most types of fish

Risotto nero

SERVES 4 AS A STARTER
1 tbsp extra-virgin olive oil
200g risotto rice (e.g. carnaroli)
25g (3 sachets) squid ink
60g butter
100g cleaned squid
1 tbsp chopped parsley

My first experience of rice black with squid ink was the *arroz negro* I enjoyed in Spain fourteen years ago. I had known about it and Italian *risotto nero*, but had never experienced either, as few London restaurants served them at that time. The version I had was sort of grey, but had a delicate flavour of the sea. Back in London, tiny sachets of squid ink were the only thing imported then. We would cut these open and boil them in the stock to get the most out of them.

1 To make the stock: melt the butter in a large saucepan and add the vegetables, bay, peppercorns, fennel, thyme and garlic. Cover and cook gently for 5 minutes, stirring occasionally, until the vegetables are soft.

2 Add the fish bones, squid ink and white wine, and just enough water to cover. Bring to the boil, skim off any scum that forms and simmer for 40-50 minutes. Strain the stock through a fine-meshed sieve. It should have a good, strong flavour; if not, reduce it a little. Keep it hot until you make the risotto, or if you are making the stock in advance, reheat it when you are ready to use it.

3 To make the risotto: heat the olive oil in a heavy-bottomed saucepan, add the rice and stir over a low heat for a couple of minutes, without allowing it to colour. Add the squid ink, stir well and then slowly add the hot stock, a ladleful or two at a time, ensuring that all the liquid has been absorbed before adding more and stirring constantly.

4 When the rice is tender, add half the butter and a little more stock if the risotto seems a bit dry. It should be wet but not runny.

5 Cut the squid into rough 1cm dice and fry it in the remaining butter for 1-2 minutes, seasoning and turning them frequently. Scatter them over the risotto with the parsley to serve.

Variations

You can, of course, just make the risotto with the ink but without the squid garnish - as it is often served in Italy and Spain. You can also use this basic recipe, minus the squid ink, to make all sorts of shellfish risotti. I particularly love risotto with langoustines - or Dublin bay prawns, as they are sometimes known - and samphire. Cook 1kg live langoustines or large raw prawns in boiling salted water for 2 minutes. Drain and let cool, then remove the heads and peel off the tail shells. Put the meat in the fridge until ready to serve and use the shells in the stock instead of the fish bones. Give the stock a good colour by adding a pinch of saffron strands and a tablespoon of tomato purée. Add 100g trimmed and washed samphire and a tablespoon of double cream at the end with the shellfish meat.

for the stock
good knob of butter
1 onion, roughly chopped
1 leek, roughly chopped and well rinsed
1 bay leaf
10 black peppercorns
1/2 tsp fennel seeds
sprig of thyme
2 garlic cloves, chopped
1 kg fish bones, rinsed and chopped
20g squid ink (2-3 sachets)
1/2 glass of white wine

OTHER SUITABLE FISH: cuttlefish

Fried soft-shell crabs with carrot & coriander salad

SERVES 4

4 soft-shell crabs, each about
50g, or larger if you wish

vegetable or corn oil, for deep-
frying

for the batter

1 egg yolk

200ml iced water

50g plain flour

50g potato flour

for the carrot and coriander salad

6 medium carrots, peeled and
finely shredded

4 spring onions, finely shredded
at an angle

2 tsp sweet chilli sauce

1 tbsp rice vinegar

2 tbsp chopped coriander

salt and freshly ground black
pepper

Soft-shell crabs are a weird phenomenon, although it is quite natural for a crab to lose its shell in order to grow – and the new shell, as it develops, is soft enough to cook and eat. I remember once being offered soft-shell lobsters by my fishmonger, which I couldn't resist. I fried them in the same way as the crabs here and they too were totally delicious. If you can't get fresh soft-shell crabs from your fishmonger, you can usually find them frozen in Oriental supermarkets.

1 Make the batter by mixing the ingredients together, but don't worry if there are a few lumps left in it.

2 Quarter the crabs and pat dry on kitchen paper. Meanwhile, preheat about 8cm of oil to 160–180°C in a deep-fryer or heavy-based pan.

3 Make the salad by mixing the carrots with the spring onions, chilli sauce, vinegar and coriander, and season with salt and pepper. Set aside.

4 Dip the pieces of soft-shell crab in the batter and fry them, a few pieces at a time, for 2–3 minutes until crisp, then drain on kitchen paper.

5 Pile the carrot salad on plates with the soft-shell crab and serve immediately.

OTHER SUITABLE FISH: other soft-shelled shellfish, such as lobster, shelled prawns and scallops

Index

A

aïoli, 50
  roasted shellfish with, 126
American seafood sauce, 150
anchovies, beetroot salad with, 26
asparagus: lobster and asparagus cocktail, 57
  tempura prawns and, 145

B

baking fish, 118
barbecuing fish, 31
batter coating, 83
béarnaise sauce, 33
beer batter, 83
beetroot salad with anchovies, 26
bisque, shellfish, 40
black bean sauce, steamed scallops and tiger
  prawns with, 122
black pudding, scallops with girolles,
  mousseline potato and, 93
bottarga, spaghetti with, 23
brandade, 79
bread: croutons, 50
  grilled flutes, 50
  pana catalana, 50
broad beans: monkfish fillets with summer
  vegetables, 109
  razor clams with chorizo and, 148
burgers, prawn, 96
butter, herb, 31
butterflying prawns, 12

C

cabbage: Alsacienne cabbage, 106
  colcannon, 88
capers: skate with black butter and, 27
  tartare sauce, 83, 96
carrot and coriander salad, 156
Catalan fish stew, 47
caviar: eggs royale, 129
ceviche, fish, 20
chicken: chicken and crayfish pies, 102-3
  paella, 100
chickpeas, grilled squid with pancetta and, 37
chillies: barbecued prawns piri piri, 34
  chilli salsa, 31
Chinese greens, seared mackerel with, 105
chorizo, steamed razor clams with broad
  beans and, 148
clams, 14
  spaghetti alle vongole, 61
  steamed razor clams with chorizo and
    broad beans, 148
cockles, 14
  pollack with samphire and, 113
cod chitterlings, 15
cod's tongues, 15
colcannon, 88
cooking techniques, 29-31, 81-3, 118
crab, 12-13
  clear tomato jelly with, 49

dressing, 13
  fried soft-shell crabs with carrot and
    coriander salad, 156
  spiced baked spider crab, 94
crayfish: chicken and crayfish pies, 102-3
  pike with sauce nantua, 140
croutons, 50
cucumber, pickled, 67
cullen skink, 52
curries: fish curry, 78
  kedgeree, 77
cuttlefish, 14

D

deep-frying, 81-3
dogfish: rock eel bordelaise, 139
Dover sole with béarnaise sauce, 33
dressings, 62

E

eels in green sauce, 91
eggs: egg and breadcrumb coating, 83
  eggs royale, 129
  kedgeree, 77
  omelette Arnold Bennett, 130
  poached turbot with egg sauce, 138
  scrambled eggs with smoked salmon, 17
  smoked haddock with poached egg and
    colcannon, 88
elvers, 64
en papillote, baking fish, 118

F

fennel: rare seared tuna with shaved fennel
  salad, 75
filleting fish, 8-9
fish curry, 78
fish fingers, 89
fish heads, 15
fish pie, 99
fish soup, 53
fish tagine, 108
fishcakes, 80
flat fish, filleting, 9
fritters: fritto misto di mare, 97
  haddock specials, 84

G

garlic: aïoli, 50
gherkins: tartare sauce, 83, 96
gravadlax, 71
griddling fish, 29-31
grilling fish, 29
gumbo, shrimp and okra, 42

H

haddock: haddock specials, 84
  see also smoked haddock
herb butter, 31
herring roes, see roes
herrings: herrings with Alsacienne cabbage,
  106
  herring salad, 90
hollandaise sauce, 129

J

John Dory with baby leeks, 112

K

kedgeree, 77

L

langoustines, 9, 12
  paella, 100
  spring vegetable minestrone with, 46
leeks: John Dory with baby leeks, 112
  vichyssoise with oysters, 41
lemon: fish ceviche, 20
lime: fish ceviche, 20
liver, monkfish, 15
lobster, 12
  lobster and asparagus cocktail, 57
  lobster with sweetbreads and tarragon, 142
  sea bass with lobster mash, 131

M

mackerel with stir-fried Chinese greens, 105
marinades, 31
mayonnaise, 62
  aïoli, 50
  tartare sauce, 83, 96
  wasabi mayonnaise, 153
minestrone, spring vegetable with langoustines,
  46
monkfish: Catalan fish stew, 47
  fish tagine, 108
  monkfish fillets with summer vegetables, 109
  Thai fish and coconut soup, 55
monkfish liver, 15
mouclade, 39
moules marinière, 124
mushrooms: rock eel bordelaise, 139
  scallops with black pudding, girolles and
    mousseline potato, 93
  sea trout with mousserons, 70
mussels, 13-14
  Catalan fish stew, 47
  mouclade, 39
  moules marinière, 124
  paella, 100

N

nantua sauce, 102-3

O

octopus and potato salad, 60
okra and shrimp gumbo, 42
omelette Arnold Bennett, 130
oysters, 149-50
  fried oysters in angel hair, 153
  opening, 150
  oysters Rockefeller, 152
  vichyssoise with, 41

P

paella, 100
pana catalana, 50
pancetta, grilled squid with chickpeas and, 37
parsley: pollack with parsley sauce, 28

skate in parsleyed jelly, 66-7
pasta: spaghetti alle vongole, 61
    spaghetti with bottarga, 23
pâté, herring roe, 90
pea purée, minted, 83
pickled cucumber, 67
pies: chicken and crayfish pies, 102-3
    fish pie, 99
pike with sauce nantua, 140
plaice belle meunière, 136
pollack: fish pie, 99
    with parsley sauce, 28
    with samphire and cockles, 113
pork-stuffed sea bream with ginger sauce,
    133
potatoes: brandade, 79
    fish pie, 99
    fishcakes, 80
    haddock specials, 84
    hot-smoked salmon with horseradish
        potatoes, 137
    octopus and potato salad, 60
    scallops with black pudding, girolles and
        mousseline potato, 93
    sea bass with lobster mash, 131
    smoked haddock with poached egg and
        colcannon, 88
    vichyssoise with oysters, 41
potted shrimps on toast, 58
prawns: butterflying, 12
    deveining, 12
    fish pie, 99
    fritto misto di mare, 97
    prawn burgers, 96
    prawns piri piri, 34
    salt and pepper tiger prawns, 120
    shrimp and okra gumbo, 42
    steamed scallops and tiger prawns with
        black bean sauce, 122
    tempura prawns and asparagus, 145
preparing fish, 8-14
preserving fish, 15

R

red mullet and samphire salad, 72
rice: kedgeree, 77
    paella, 100
    risotto nero, 154-5
roasting fish, 118
rock eel bordelaise, 139
roes, 15
    herring roes on toast, 65
    herring salad, 90
    plaice belle meunière, 136
    spaghetti with bottarga, 23
rouille, 53
round fish, filleting, 9

S

salads, 62
    beetroot salad with anchovies, 26
    fried soft-shell crabs with carrot and
        coriander salad, 156
    grilled sardines with Essaouira salad, 107

herring salad, 90
    octopus and potato salad, 60
    rare seared tuna with shaved fennel salad,
        75
    red mullet and samphire salad, 72
    salade niçoise, 74
    sashimi of scallops with seaweed salad, 121
    seafood salad, 125
salmon: fish pie, 99
    gravadlax, 71
    kedgeree, 77
    salmon tartare, 22
    see also smoked salmon
salsas: chilli salsa, 31
    salsa verde, 31
salt and pepper tiger prawns, 120
salt-baked sea bass, 114-15
salt cod, brandade, 79
salting fish, 15
samphire: octopus and potato salad with, 60
    pollack with cockles and, 113
    red mullet and samphire salad, 72
    seafood salad, 125
sardines with Essaouira salad, 107
sashimi, 18-19
    scallops with seaweed salad, 121
sauces, 62
    American seafood, 150
    béarnaise, 33
    bordelaise, 139
    cocktail, 57
    curry, 77
    dill mustard, 71
    dipping, 117
    egg, 138
    ginger, 133
    hollandaise, 129
    nantua, 102-3
    quick pan sauce, 118
    tartare, 83, 96
scallops: sashimi of scallops with seaweed
    salad, 121
    scallops thermidor, 143
    scallops with black pudding, girolles and
        mousseline potato, 93
    steamed scallops and tiger prawns with
        black bean sauce, 122
sea bass: fish ceviche, 20
    salt-baked sea bass, 114-15
    sea bass with lobster mash, 131
sea bream: Catalan fish stew, 47
    pork-stuffed sea bream with ginger sauce,
        133
sea trout with mousserons, 70
seafood salad, 125
seafood sauce, American, 150
seaweed salad, sashimi of scallops with, 121
shallot vinegar, 150
shellfish, 9-14
    roasted shellfish with aïoli, 126
    shellfish bisque, 40
shrimps: plaice belle meunière, 136
    potted shrimps on toast, 58
    shrimp and okra gumbo, 42

see also prawns
skate: skate in parsleyed jelly, 66-7
    skate with black butter and capers, 27
smoked haddock: cullen skink, 52
    kedgeree, 77
    omelette Arnold Bennett, 130
    smoked haddock with poached egg and
        colcannon, 88
smoked salmon: eggs royale, 129
    hot-smoked salmon with horseradish
        potatoes, 137
    scrambled eggs with, 17
sole with béarnaise sauce, 33
soups, 38-55
    accompaniments, 50
    Catalan fish stew, 47
    clear tomato jelly with crab, 49
    cullen skink, 52
    fish soup, 53
    mouclade, 39
    shellfish bisque, 40
    shrimp and okra gumbo, 42
    spring vegetable minestrone with
        langoustines, 46
    Thai fish and coconut soup, 55
    vichyssoise with oysters, 41
spaghetti alle vongole, 61
spaghetti with bottarga, 23
spring vegetable minestrone with
    langoustines, 46
squid, 14
    Catalan fish stew, 47
    fritto misto di mare, 97
    grilled squid with chickpeas and pancetta, 37
    risotto nero, 154-5
stew, Catalan fish, 47
storing fish, 8
sweetbreads, lobster with tarragon and, 142

T

tagine, fish, 108
tartare sauce, 83, 96
tempura batter, 83
tempura prawns and asparagus, 145
Thai baked fish, 117
Thai fish and coconut soup, 55
tomatoes: clear tomato jelly with crab, 49
    tomato vinaigrette, 72
tuna: rare seared tuna with shaved fennel
    salad, 75
    salade niçoise, 74
turbot with egg sauce, 138

V

vichyssoise with oysters, 41
vinaigrette, 62
    tomato vinaigrette, 72
vinegar, shallot, 150

W

watercress: eels in green sauce, 91

Y

yeast batter, 83

Where to buy fish, etc.

London
Blagdens Fishmongers
65 Paddington Street,
London W1M 3RR
tel 020 7935 8321
email blagfish@vossnet.co.uk

Chalmers and Gray
67 Notting Hill Gate, ,
London W11 3JS
tel 020 7221 6177

Furness Fish and Poultry
Borough Market,
8 Southwark Street,
London SE1 1TL
tel 7407 1002

The Good Harvest Fish and
Meat Market (Oriental specialist)
14 Newport Place,
London WC2H 7PR
tel 020 7437 0712

Kensington Place Fish Shop
199a Kensington Church Street,
London W8 7LX
tel 020 7243 6626

Steve Hatt
88-90 Essex Road,
London N1 8LU
tel 020 7226 3963

North of England
Cross of York
3 & 4 Newgate Market, York,
North Yorkshire YO1 7LA
tel: 01904 551355 (24-hour
answerphone)
email: york.market@york.gov.uk

Direct Fish
28-30 Bridge Street Brow,
Stockport SK1 1XY
tel 0161 480 2841
Also at Withenshawe Market: tel
0161 437 7588 and Arndale
Centre, High Street,
Manchester M4 2EB
tel 0161 832 8908

Alfred Enderby Ltd
(Smokehouse)
Fish Dock Road, Fish Docks,
Grimsby,
North East Lincolnshire DN31 3NE
tel 01472 342 984
www.alfredenderby.co.uk

West Country
Phil Bowditch
7 Bath Place, Taunton,
Somerset TA1 4ER
tel 01823 253500

Fish Works
6 Green Street,
Bath,
Avon BA1 2JY
tel 01225 447794

Dennis Knight
1 Fore Street,
Port Isaac,
Devon PL29 3RB
tel 01208 880498

Martins Seafresh
St Columb Business Centre,
Barn Lane, St Columb,
Cornwall TR9 6BU
tel 0800 0272066
www.martins-seafresh.co.uk
sales@martins-seafresh.co.uk

Samways
Station Road, West Bay,
Dorset DT6 4EN
tel 01308 424 496

Steins Seafood Deli
South Quay, Padstow,
Cornwall PL28 8BL
tel 01841 533466

South Coast
Burts Butchers & Fishmongers
49 George Street, Hove,
East Sussex BN3 3YB
tel 01273 731407

Rock-a-Nore Fisheries
3 Rock-a-Nore Road,
Hastings,
East Sussex TN34 3DW
tel 01424 445 425

Ireland
Ballycotton Seafood
46 Main St, Midleton,
Co Cork
tel 00 353 21 461 3122
www.ballycottonseafood.com

Mortons
9 Bayview Road. Ballycastle,
Co Antrim BT54 6BP
tel 028 2076 2348

Wales
Ashtons
Central Market, Cardiff,
South Glamorgan CF10 2AU
tel 029 2022 9201

Coakley Greene
Stall 41c, The Market,
Oxford Street,
Swansea,
West Glamorgan SA1 3PF
tel 01792 653416

Scotland
Anchor Seafoods
The Pier, Portree,
Isle Of Skye 1V51 9DE
tel 01478 612 414

Alex Spink & Sons, (World
famous for their smoked fish)
24 Seagate (office),
Arbroath, DD11 1BJ
tel 01241 879056

Alan Beveridge
188 Byres Road,
Glasgow G12 8SN
tel 0141 357 2766

Eddie's Seafood Market
7 Roseneath Street,
Edinburgh EH9 1JH
tel 0131 229 4207

Andrew Keracher
5-8 Whitefriars Street,
Perth PH1 1PP
tel 01738 638454

MacCallums
71 Houldsworth Street,
Glasgow G3 8ED
tel 0141 2044456

Mail Order Suppliers
Abbotsbury Oysters
(Oyster knives available; other
shellfish available on request)
Ferryman's Way, Ferrybridge,
Weymouth Dorset. DT4 9YA
tel 01305 788867

Brown and Forrest Ltd (Smoked
eel and salmon)
FREEPOST S 6843, Langport
Somerset TA10 0BP
tel: 01458 250 875
www.smokedeel.co.uk

Cuan Sea Fisheries Ltd. (Oysters)
Sketrick Island, Killinchy,
Newtownards
Co Down, Northern Ireland.
tel 028 97 541 461 and
020 7732 0500/3144
email:cuan.oysters@virgin.net
wwwcuanoysters.com

Forman and Field
(Smoked and fresh fish, caviar
and other cooked and preserved
products)
30a Marshgate Lane,
London E15 2NH
tel 020 8221 3939
www.formanandfield.com

Hebridean Smokehouse Ltd
(Lots of quality and interesting
smoked fish)
Clachan, Locheport,
Isle of North Uist
tel 01876 580 209
www.hebrideansmokehouse.com

Loch Fyne Oysters Ltd
(Oysters, smoked fish, cured
products)
tel 01499 600264
www.loch-fyne.com

Mathew Stevens & Son
(Local and imported fish and
shellfish, smoked fish)
Back Road East, St Ives,
Cornwall TR26 1NW
tel 01736 799 392
www.mstevensandson.com

Princesse d'Isenbourg et Cie
(Luxury fish products, fresh
Iranian caviar, smoked salmon,
and lots of other fish and non-
fish goodies)
2 Bard Rd, London W10 6TP
tel 020 8960 3600
www.caviar.co.uk

Useful Organizations
Marine Stewardship Council
www.msc.org

Marine Conservation Society
tel 01989 566 017
www.mcsuk.org

Ocean Trust
www.oceantrust.org

Acknowledgements

The author would like to thank all those who worked on the book. As always the quality of the team you choose to work with pays dividends and, as with cooking, a book will benefit from key players and good ingredients. Thanks to Vanessa Courtier for putting up with Jason Lowe and myself on long fishy shoots and to Lewis Esson for dotting the 'i's and editing my waffle and stuff. Thanks also to Jane O' Shea for commissioning the book in the first place. Along the way, Lee Bull made life very much easier by chopping and filleting and fetching things I had forgotten to order. Angela Boggiano ably filled in all the gaps when I just couldn't miss a meeting.

Les Ironman at Southbank Seafoods did well to keep up with replacing sea trout when heads were out and tails were in, as did Tony Booth in sourcing those last-minute peculiar veggies when the season was almost over or the weather destroyed the crop. Finally, thanks to Revol for their china, as supplied by David Alexander at Pages of Shaftesbury Avenue.